Sonia Baeriswyl

Coach yourself to success

Createspace 2018

Disclaimer

The information contained in "Coach Yourself To Success." and its components, is meant to serve as a comprehensive collection of strategies that the author of this eBook has done research about. Summaries, strategies, tips and tricks are only recommendations by the author, and reading this eBook will not guarantee that one's results will exactly mirror the author's results.

The author of this Ebook has made all reasonable efforts to provide current and accurate information for the readers of this eBook. The author and its associates will not be held liable for **any** unintentional errors or omissions that may be found.

The material in the Ebook may include information by third parties. Third party materials comprise of opinions expressed by their owners. As such, the author of this eBook does not assume responsibility or liability for any third party material or opinions.

The publication of third party material does not constitute the author's guarantee of any information, products, services, or opinions contained within third party material. Use of third party material does not guarantee that your results will mirror our results. Publication of such third party material is simply a recommendation and expression of the author's own opinion of that material.

Whether because of the progression of the Internet, or the unforeseen changes in company policy and editorial submission guidelines, what is stated as fact at the time of this writing may become outdated or inapplicable later.

This Ebook is copyright © 2017 by Sonia Baeriswyl with all rights reserved. It is illegal to redistribute, copy, or create derivative works from this Ebook whole or in parts. No parts of this report may be reproduced or retransmitted in any forms whatsoever with the written expressed and signed permission from the author.

Table of contents

Chapter 1: Love yourself, self esteem..................................7
  Your self esteem is your responsibility..........................10
Chapter 2: The key to loving yourself.................................12
  Feel the fear..14
    The intersection of fear and excitement............................16
    Do a trial run 17
    Just do it..17
  Do what you love..17
    Live what you love... 17
  Nothing is impossible just make a full effort...................21
    Disk or sphere 21
    There is much more than we can see 21
    How can we make our wish more likely? 22
    Knowing what you want... 22
Chapter 3: Mind power..24
    What is mind power? 24
  Your mind power is your destiny..................................25
    Why is it so? 26
  A balanced body for a balanced mind...........................27
  6 easy to follow tips to improve mind power.................29
    Practice, practice, practice 29
    Improve mind power through a healthy diet 29
    Snooze your way to improve mind power 30
    Improve brain power through mental stimulation 30
    Journals and blogging to improve mind power 30
    Improve brain power through human interaction............ 30

How to differentiate fear from intuition........................31
　What is intuition?...31
Eight ways your intuition talks to you........................35
8 ways to sharpen your intuition and make your life better...36
　Self love 36
　Listen to your body... 36
　Embrace quietness 37
　Sit with your problem... 37
　Play games with your intuition 37
　Ask intuition based questions 38
　Follow your intuitive hunches... 38
　Journal 39

Chapter 4: Detachment the key to getting what you desire.40
　Attachment... 40
　Detachment 41
Get what you want..42
Goal setting-how to get what you want..............................43
　Select a goal 44
　Put a time on it 44
　Amount of money needed 44
　Time investment... 44
7 secrets of using what you've got to get what you want...45
　Start slow take baby steps 45
　Persistence 45
　Assertive self starter 45
　Present mindedness 45
　Independence... 46
　Ability to fail constructively 46

 Ability to shake discouragement 46
Manifest what you desire into reality................................**46**
Manifest desires get what you want..................................**48**
Chapter 5: Ask, believe, receive..**50**
 Create a picture of what you want..50
 Express your needs...50
 Pick right time for conversation...51
 Here's how to ask, believe & receive....................................51
 Five hidden benefits that come from asking to receive...52
  Humility 52
  Allowing others to receive blessings 52
  Leading by example.. 53
  Helping others help us 53
  The creator can help us through other people 53
Chapter 6: Power of focus..**54**
  You get what you focus on..55
  Focus as it relates to our use of time..................................57
  Focus: follow one course until successful 58
The law of attraction and the power of focus..................**60**
Give yourself the gift of time..**61**
  Time is eternal... 63
Chapter 7: Comfort zone...**65**
  Why don't we step outside our comfort zones more often?....... 68
  A quick guide to stepping outside your comfort zone................ 69
Humility a true greatness..**70**
  Why is humility better than tolerance?........................... 70
  Humility divine perspective 72
  Definition 72
  Inner bases of humility 73

- External bases of humility 74
- Individual life & humility 75
- Collective life & humility 75
- Entrepreneurship & humility 76

5 keys to cultivate humility in life, love, and leadership .. 77

Chapter 8: The courage to live consciously 78

- Dimensions of courage 78

Tips to boost your courage 80

Bad habits and self sabotage 83

No more excuses 86

- Get in touch with your deepest desires 86
- Eliminate if's and but's 87
- The time is now 87
- What it takes to win 87
- Setting a standard 87

Wake up 88

- Waking up with determination sets the pace 89
- Being determined by small changes 89
- Waking up with determination is a choice 90

The key to wake up with determination 90

- Determination is also taking risks 90
- Risk and the will to win 90

Determination is essential 91

- Being determined builds momentum 91

4 steps to wake up with determination 92

A final word 93

Chapter 1
Love yourself, self esteem

Self-esteem issues seem to be one of the most influential emotions that challenge many people today. It has become humanity first worry when she awakens, and her last worry before she sleeps.

Self-Esteem comes from the Latin word which means to Estimate, so Self-Esteem is how you would Estimate yourself.

Self-Esteem effects how you look at yourself in the mirror; feel and talk about yourself, it's important to know who you are and to value yourself.

Self-Esteem knows that you are worth a lot (priceless) but not bragging about how good you are, its how much you value yourself and how important you feel about your achievements, nobody is perfect but knowing that you worthy of being loved and accepted.

There are a number of people who are confident, when they fall into the public eye, such as politicians, actors, comedians, artists and the like, they seem to glow with assertiveness, some of these individuals, although they are attractive and world famous, they find it hard to value themselves, they feel insecure, and they lack in self-esteem.

So what is self-esteem? It is not the same as confidence, that's for sure!

So self-esteem means:

- To value yourself highly without being pretentious
- To have a positive attitude
- Being confident in what you do
- Liking yourself for who you are
- Be deserving of love and happiness
- Being a good human being and taking criticism as constructive to help you become a better person
- You feel OK in both mind and body

If you suffer from low self-esteem, you will struggle to associate the above with yourself, and you will lack self-assurance and self-respect.

Self-Esteem is essential in knowing what you can do, be proud of yourself and hold your head up high, and it gives you the courage to try new things and to believe, respect and Pamper yourself.

To be low on self-esteem means to not think highly of yourself and to criticise yourself too much, if you have little self-esteem you may not always think good of yourself, and you believe that you are not important.

It is said that we are all born with natural self-esteem, but through the concerns of the world about power and control, we have been trained to worry about what others think of us and how we can please them. We have forgotten how to love ourselves and treat ourselves with respect. We are taught that loving ourselves is selfish and will only make us appear conceited, which will turn people off. If we are not allowed to learn how to love ourselves, then how can we learn to allow others to love us? We cannot feel love and positive esteem for ourselves if we focus all of it on others first. If we do, we then run the risk of offering all of our inner feelings to someone and not getting anything in return. At this point, we begin to feel resentment, cheated and even lower in our ability to ever love again.

People that have scars from resentment and abuse are the hardest people to love. They have the highest low self-esteem walls to climb. In short, they are unreachable. It is not a good thing at all.

When a person says in all honesty that they are suffering from a low self-esteem issue, this is an issue that needs to be taken seriously. It is a genuine cry for help. They are at the bottom of their pit and are asking for help to get out. They are at a point where they will expect you to love them and take care of them as they would themselves. In other words, we all know the worst thing a person can do is expect their partner to be a mind reader. Well, when a person is suffering from low self-esteem, trust me, they do expect just that. They will wait you just to know what they need. They only have faith in you. They have lost faith in themselves long ago, and they have no recourse. It places a significant burden on your shoulders as their partner. It is not a good thing!

No one will ever be able to feel what another person feels inside. No one will ever be able to love another as they can love themselves. No one can read our minds. No one can do for us, what needs to be done to make us feel inner peace. It is our responsibility to ourselves to love us first. You really must know who you are to start. To be able to fulfil your needs and desires and goals in life, you need to identify with your wants. You cannot do any of this if you do not focus on you. You need to be all about you for a time. No one can do this for you, so just do it!

It is called finding your space. Your space is a very, very important place just to find yourself in peace with no distractions. Only you and your thoughts. Learning about your self-esteem also means that you must come to terms with this question, "How badly do you want to have higher self-esteem"? If you want it, then you will find it. You have been trained to un-love yourself, so it is not impossible to retrain yourself to love you again. Your environment is also essential in helping you feel positive vibes. For you to indeed accept yourself unconditionally, you must look beyond the simple, quick fix motto's that are plaguing television and magazines, such as diets that will make you a better you or take this pill, and you will be a new you. Ugh, there are so many misconceptions out there. It seriously boils down to your mind and your heart. Love yourself as you want to be loved. Love yourself as you want to love someone! Just be you! That is a perfect thing!

Remember, "HABITS"? Well, that's exactly what you need to do. Create loving you habits and respecting your habits. Think of it as your very first self-esteem day. You wake up, you stretch and hug your partner or just yourself. Even hugging your pillow is a good hug. You have no memory of any other feelings. You love yourself. You have no other intention but to take care of you. You look in the mirror and stick your tongue out and roll your eyes inward and smile! Smile at you because you love who you are. It's an excellent thing to be able to laugh at you for no other reason than it is good to be you!

Please do not get it wrong here. Life will still challenge you with its ups and downs. You will still have to deal with all the negative things that your day will unravel. But the difference is, you will be doing it from bright, fresh, confident self-esteem eyes. Nothing will defeat you in the end. Oh, it may give you a run for your money, but you will override all of it with your smiles and love for yourself. Imagine the confidence that will shine inside of you. Your reactions will be out of love and understanding. They will no longer be from resentment and hate. It is a good thing!

Remember also that anything worth having does not come quickly. Once it has been attained or learned, it remains forever. This too is a good thing! Many women have experienced the highs and the lows of self-esteem, you are so not alone in this battle to find a better you! To finally have the gift of self-confidence will not bring you happiness, that is something that comes after. But it will bring you a deep awareness of who you are. New respect for you. A genuine love for yourself and the confidence to soar! Finding your self-esteem saves your world, not anyone else's. But it does give you the strength to help others to find theirs.

Your self esteem is your responsibility

It is true that your self-esteem is shaped by how parents, teachers, peers and others treat us during our upbringing, but you cannot blame these people if you have low self-esteem now. When you blame others, you disempower yourself. If you dis-empower yourself, you will never raise your self-esteem although you CAN increase it if you take full personal responsibility.

Your self-esteem is not affected by what others do to you. It is affected by how you interpret what others do to you. If somebody criticises you, you can understand this as that you are wrong or as that the person is having a bad day. Thus, even if you are bullied by your colleagues, your family has deserted you or your friends are abusing you, you still cannot blame low self-esteem on them. You are responsible for your thoughts and feelings about yourself, and these thoughts and feelings are what make up your self-esteem. You can choose to think positive thoughts about yourself and thereby improve your opinions as well. Self-esteem is a choice.

The self-esteem that you built up during your childhood provides the base on which your present self-esteem is built. It does not mean that you have to keep low self-esteem that you developed as a child because of negative events that happened to you. The past is in the history and what is important is what kind of self-esteem you want to have NOW. If you choose to and stay committed to raising your self-esteem, the negative things that others have done to you in the past will not matter. When you take responsibility for your thoughts, nobody will be able to stop you from raising your self-esteem.

If you do not take responsibility for your self-esteem and instead blame others, you will never be anything more than a puppet. Your happiness and success with merely be a matter of luck, always depending on what others do to you. Instead of achieving your goals, you will be used by others to attaining their goals.

Chapter 2
The key to loving yourself

It is imperative for one to love himself. When you don't love yourself, it is hard to expect others to love you. Agreed, we may have many faults and shortcomings. But you must embrace yourself with all your faults and learn to love yourself.

Self-love and self-esteem are related to each other. If you suffer from low esteem, you can't have enough self-love. With low confidence, you will find it hard to love yourself at first, because you don't think highly of yourself. But as you start loving yourself, your self-esteem will be boosted, and you'll have higher confidence.

If you want to love yourself, you need to make a conscious decision. It is a decision that you have to make for a fulfilled and happy life. With low self-esteem, you can never reach your full potential. It is, therefore, a crucial 'task' to love yourself.

Here are some tips that will help you complete this task

Understand yourself: If you want your personality to grow, you need to understand yourself and know what makes you bloom. You may have many flaws, but you need to accept them and move on. You should know that nobody is perfect. Yes, even the most perfect person you have met or idolised also has flaws. You are not the only one. Go ahead and stand in front of a mirror. Admire your reflection and fall in love with yourself. You might not be as important for others, but in your life story, you are the hero, and your life revolves around you.

Don't criticise yourself: Do you belittle yourself over small things? Whenever you make any little mistake, do you get a voice inside your head telling you that you are stupid and good for nothing? If that happens a lot with you, you need to stop criticising yourself. It is essential to look at your positive points instead of focusing on the negative ones.

Be positive and kind: When you start thinking positive, you become more sympathetic towards yourself and your self-love increases. With this, increases your self-esteem and confidence.

Kindness towards others also helps. You need to love other people. If you feel general hatred towards others, you'll turn out to be a bitter person, and this will decrease your love towards yourself. Love others and try to help them. It will make you feel better about yourself, and you'll love yourself easily.

Acknowledge your efforts: You might not have succeeded, but at least you have made efforts. Many people in the world never make any efforts. If you made honest efforts about something but were unable to succeed because of any reason, don't let that bring you down. Making an effort is a big thing. It is not always about winning- sometimes, it's the effort that counts.

Don't worry: Your worries are the biggest let-downs of your life. Sometimes people don't even make an effort because they are worried that if they fail, it will not look good. Just put your worries aside. Your worries won't also let you prosper. If you want to taste success in your life, you need to stop worrying and make honest efforts.

Forgive yourself: We all make mistakes. You also made some mistakes. If you are holding on to your mistakes and thinking bad about yourself, you are making a huge mistake again. Everyone makes mistakes. Learn to forgive yourself. Unless and until you don't forgive yourself, you will not be able to come out of your past and be successful. You must believe in yourself and know that whatever was done was not intentional. Also, you must convince yourself that you have learned a lesson and that mistake will not be repeated.

Try to be spiritual: You might be an atheist, but the truth is, if you believe in a divine power, you get hope in life. You might not agree to a religion, and you don't have to- it's your choice. Just by believing that the universe takes care of things, you can let your worries go. Spirituality reduces pessimism and bitterness. If you are ever stressed out, just relax and think how big the universe is, and how unimportant we all are. Take the course of meditation. Meditation will relax your nerves, and you'll start loving yourself soon.

Be thankful: Be thankful for whatever life gives you. Not everyone gets full meals. Not everyone has access to a computer and internet... or a job... or a loving family. Just be thankful for what life has given you. This way you will appreciate the small things you have, and this will help you love yourself. You are physically fit and mentally sound.

Not everyone has it enjoy the blessings of life. Understand that you are lucky that you have all that.

Pamper yourself: Life is so busy, and as mothers, we spend so much time tending to the needs of others and pampering others that we sometimes neglect to indulge ourselves.

1. Buy yourself something pretty. You might be a fan of jewellery and flowers. Note, it doesn't have to be especially pricey. You can find a bouquet of flowers at the grocery store for under $5. And, "fashion jewellery" may seem trendy, but if you think it's pretty...go for it!
2. Do something to make you feel better about your body. Take a bubble bath, paint your toes, pluck your eyebrows...do something to pamper that body of yours.
3. About that body. Are you one of those "negative-self-talkers?" One of the best ways to pamper yourself is to STOP that right now. Stop that negative gibber-jabber.
4. Perhaps you've heard of a gratitude journal. It's a beautiful way to make yourself aware of 3 good things that happened to you throughout the day. Use this same idea for an I Love Me journal. Take some time to write 3 reasons you love yourself, every day! Point out all the beautiful things about your body, your mind, and your spirit. You can pamper yourself by loving yourself.
5. Daydream. Kids do it all the time. Go back to your child-like innocence and enjoy a lovely vision. Imagine yourself somewhere beautiful. Think pleasant thoughts. Be at one with the moment, which is currently yours.

You can pamper yourself. You can take just a few minutes each day to appreciate and love yourself. Take care of yourself, and everyone in your life will be better off.

Feel the fear

Feeling fear whenever you are thrusting yourself outside your comfort zone is a natural response. The challenge is to know when fear is justified and a reason to stop or when concern is just a regular part of the success journey and an opportunity for you to use the fear to sharpen your senses, where you confront the fear and go ahead anyway.

When fear is justified, for example where you may be entering into a contractual agreement with someone that is less than trustworthy, it is crucial to listen to your inner voice and to use the fear you feel to protect yourself. On the other hand, any time you thrust yourself into unchartered territory, where you are pushed outside your self-imposed comfort zone, you will feel fear too. The challenge is to know when fear is real and justified and when it is just your natural desire to seek comfort and avoid pain.

Super achievers have mastered this art, and they very quickly identify whether fear is justified or whether it is just a reasonable fear that they are feeling because they are taking a calculated risk and are pushing the boundaries of their comfort zone. You need to invest time to develop this art, where you can very quickly tell if fear is justified or whether it is just your natural aversion to inviting some risk into your life. Feeling fear is a physical protection mechanism that is built into your brain to protect you from any imminent danger.

The way to enter the realm of super achievement is to know whether fear is justified or not very quickly and to confront your fear, where you feel the fear and go ahead anyway or when to realise that your fear is real and you must take action to avoid the danger. You can never get rid of your fear, but you can learn the art of confronting your fear and using it to your advantage.

For example:

- Your fear of ignorance can be used to generate inspiration to grow your knowledge constantly.
- Your fear of poverty can be used to inspire you to work a little harder.
- Your fear of disease can encourage you to take better care of your body.
- The fear of losing your family can inspire you to remain faithful, work a little harder and show them love as often as possible.

The secret to becoming and remaining a super achiever is to learn the art of quickly identifying the difference between mortal or justified fear or helpful fear or unjustified fear. As soon as you make the shift toward understanding how to use fear to your advantage you turn something that can be very limiting and restrictive into an asset that you can use to create massive success in your life.

Once you have learnt the art of knowing when fear is real and justified or when it is just a natural response to your attachment to stability, it is time to introduce the art of daily discipline into your life. As Roy L Smith said, "Discipline is the refining fire by which talent becomes ability." Regular training is the key to unlock your potential and to turn you into a high-performance human being, who operates at levels of super achievement.

Positive self-discipline, where you commit to carrying out all the tasks you need to each day, puts you firmly in the driver's seat and over time, these consistent efforts will turn into the success you desire. Yes, success does require a commitment to daily discipline and an investment of some of your valuable time, which will cost you something small each day. Failure, on the other hand, requires nothing from you each day, but the price you will pay in the long run will be massive. What choice do you want to make with your future?

You have probably heard the phrase, Feel the Fear and Do It Anyway. Some of you may live by that mantra. Others may feel the fear and let it paralyse them, never taking risks, living a life of safety and complacency. The concern is a natural emotion that we all feel at times, and that can keep us safe when facing danger or something that we are ill prepared for. Fear can prompt us to do more research when embarking on a new venture, and it can serve as the impetus for better planning. But fear can sometimes also stop us dead in our tracks, serving as a barrier to personal and professional growth. Is there a happy medium? Yes!

The intersection of fear and excitement

Think about something you would like to do, try, or embark on that you haven't yet because fear has reared its ugly head. For one reason or another, you have fear around trying this activity, doing this task or embarking on this journey. It makes no difference whether it is personal or professional. It could be as big as starting a new business, changing jobs, or relocating, or a smaller undertaking like starting a blog or trying a new hobby.

Now, see if you also have excitement around trying this task, activity or new journey. Can you answer yes to the excitement part? If so, great! If you were to look at this potential undertaking as a pie, how much of your reaction and emotion around doing it is fear and how much is excitement? For you to overcome the fear, there has to be some excitement to balance it out! And if excitement is a more significant piece of the pie, even better. You will be able to move forward with more confidence knowing that your enthusiasm will help guide the way and cancel out some of the fear.

What if the fear is an overwhelmingly more significant piece of the pie than excitement? Does this mean you are doomed to stay stuck forever? Not necessarily. You may not have done enough research or due diligence to get excited about it yet. Excitement often comes when we can start to actually "see" our dreams and plans take shape, and that can take more time to work out in our minds before the excitement sets in. But if you never feel any excitement about this undertaking and fear is the big black cloud hanging over this, chances are, it is either not the right path for you... or your fear is too large to overcome at this time. So then, what do you do?

Do a trial run

You can do a trial run of your undertaking but in a way that feels safer, and perhaps smaller. For example, before opening your business, spend some time interning or shadowing a professional that does what you want to do for a living. It will give you a taste of what it would be like to be a business owner doing that work before you start it. Likewise, if you want to write a book, but fear keeps holding you back, start by writing a blog or a series of articles. Usually, doing a smaller version or trial run of the undertaking will quell some of the fear and get you pumped up!

Just do it

In the words of the popular Nike advertising campaign, just do it! Yes, I mean it. Just close both eyes and dive into the deep end.

Do what you love

Live what you love

What ignites your passion? What allows you to feel completely engaged at the moment? For many of you reading this, being absorbed in your favourite hobby, sport or past-time naturally comes to mind. You might recite the countless hours spent in pursuit of that interest and the feelings associated with it.

It is no secret that we find enormous pleasure in pursuing our passion. It must be stated that your 'work' is not the only area tied to your love. Many people find sanctuary in their past-times or hobbies which bear no financial incentive other than to provide enjoyment and self-fulfilment.

"Doing what you love to do is a process of self-discovery" is what Dr Robert Anthony says in his best-selling book doing what you love, loving what you do. That process can be a short one, or it can be a very long one. The process will depend a lot on your desire to find the answer. And it can be terrifying seeking our answers to what will make us happy. Way too often we seek the advice and direction from other people. It is almost always a bad idea when trying to discover what you would love doing. As loving as other people around us maybe they have their motives, desires and ideas about how we should live our lives. And just because they think the sun rises in the east and sets in the west doesn't mean that you can't look at it as the earth turning to the south and therefore the sun merely coming into view.

Trying to explain to someone else what you would love to be doing from their perspective is often difficult. No one else will have the same outlook on life, and the meaning of it, as you do. And if those people, especially your loved ones, never had the opportunity, or were discouraged from pursuing what they love for "practical reasons" they'll have no ability or knowledge about how to support you in doing what you love. They're only reaction might be to call you a dreamer, if so, dream on.

But the dreams we are talking about are the ones that well up from deep inside you. They're not a process of our thinking they are the product of our living. Ironically doing what you will be processing of your living through a product of your thinking. The dreams you had as a child, the dreams you still think about as an adult, are useful clues about what you would love to be doing. Think about all those ideas, all those dreams. Get a piece of paper or two and start to write. Write them all down. Don't stop to analyse them or pre-judge them, just write them down. This first step isn't about trying to decide, or figure out, what might work and what won't.

The second step is about prioritising your list. It is about doing what you love, so it isn't about financial priorities, it's about life priorities. Assuming you'll make more money settling for 'this' dream rather than 'that' one that turns your crank is a big mistake. If you're going to do that, you might as well stay working where and for who are. This list and the prioritising is about your life, not your living. Doing what you love to do, not doing what you think you can make the most money at.

Dr Robert Anthony says to "Think about the person you want to be..." Prioritizing your list isn't about what you would love to be doing first and the second and third and so on. It's about narrowing your list of dreams to that one that will get you going and growing into the person you want to be, the person you already are, somewhere down inside you. How do you begin 'doing what you love'? The best choice is to write it down as a goal. Look at it every day for at least a week and think about it. Then sit down and write out a step by step plan to create that life. Small, easy steps that anyone can do, even you, regardless of how much time it may take. But rest assured, being HONESTLY committed to doing what you love in life, and for being, will get you there faster than you could hope for.

Time stands still as we're flooded with exhilaration and excitement, absorbed in our pursuit. Such activities provide mental, emotional and physical benefits to the individual. In recent times we have seen widespread culture espouse the notion of turning your passion into profits as a viable success model. It may not necessarily appeal to all people of course.

In his commencement speech at Stanford University in 2005, the late Steve Jobs imparted graduates with the following wisdom, "... and the only way to do great work is to love what you do. If you haven't found it yet, keep looking. Don't settle." While he was alluding to one's career, we can adapt this statement to reflect other aspects of our lives where our passions run deep.

So how do you live what you love? It's so nice you asked. The following points are ways to encapsulate your passion by becoming aligned with your highest potential.

1. **Become an extension of what you love:** Embody what you love in every cell of your being by becoming an extension of your passion. People who live their love can't wait to get up in the morning to spend another day immersed in their pursuit. As Steve Jobs reminds us in the earlier quote, if you haven't found it yet - don't settle. There is nothing more

meaningless and soul destroying than pursuing a life which does not resonate with your deepest self.
2. **Find purpose and passion in other areas:** As mentioned earlier that your love or passion does not have to be tied to your work. For example, many people have hobbies or interests which do not earn money, yet provides a great deal of personal satisfaction. It takes persistence and focuses on turning your passion into profits. Thankfully those who have been privileged enough to achieve this cross-over will remind you that it often comes at a price long hours, stress, health risks, family problems etc. It should not dissuade you from pursuing this path instead that you become aware of what is involved.
3. **Harmonise with your mind and body:** When you're immersed in your passion, harmony and balance are preserved in mind and body. The art of little Bonsai tree pruning can bring such a deep satisfaction and resonance to the individual as they watch their Bonsai take shape over time. People who keep tropical fish also report feeling the same connection. Cooking is also said to have the same therapeutic effect to calm the mind and body.
4. **Slow down to the speed of life:** There is a frequency called The Schumann resonances which have a frequency range of 7.83Hz which is 7 - 10 cycles per second. This frequency is also common in the EEG readings of humans and many animals. It was discovered that the dominant brainwave frequency of shamans and healers, comes close to 7.83 Hz and may at times beat in phase with the Earth's signal, thereby causing harmonic resonance. It is scientific proof that we are wired to synchronise with the speed and frequency of life.
5. **Transcend your fears:** Move through your fears. Fear is a debilitating emotion which discolours your perception of life. It shapes your inner domain and external reality. Let go of your fears by transforming them into peace, love, faith and trust. As you let go of fear you will naturally fall in love with life. You cannot appreciate life when your mind and body are gripped by fear; which is a lower state of consciousness. Love reflects a higher state of knowledge (logarithmic level - 500) as shown on the map of consciousness whereas fear is depicted as (logarithmic scale - 100).
6. **Look for the good in all situations:** Orientate your senses to look for the positive in all conditions - not in a Pollyanna type of way. Remember the concept of duality? - Yin and yang

are parts of the whole. Therefore what may appear as a bad situation also contains the seed of something positive. As you widen your vista, you'll naturally begin to look for the good in all cases. It won't come looking for you holding up a placard, screaming to get your attention. Look for evidence in the smallest details, and you'll find it.

7. **Engage in loving relationships**: Engage in loving relationships and let go of toxic ones. Remember, we coach others how to treat us. If you are not receiving the respect you deserve, on some unconscious level, you may have attracted this relationship with you. Learn from it by going inward to dissolve any conflicts. Many people's perception of life is discoloured by their view of intimate relationships. They fail to acknowledge that life is a mirror reflecting back one's inner landscape as within, so without. As you heal your wounds, life confesses your openness to living a life vested in love.

Nothing is impossible just make a full effort

We can only see as far as the horizon goes. What lies beyond, is like some unknown space. Therefore, we might be tempted to believe that there is nothing beyond the horizon. We tend to ignore the possibilities that lie beyond our perceived horizon.

Disk or sphere

For a long, long time, humankind believed that the earth was a disk instead of a ball. They only knew what was called "the Old World" back then, which consisted of continental Europe and some parts of Africa and Asia. It was just around 500 years ago that our ancestors learned that there is more than the Old World and that the earth is a sphere.

There is much more than we can see

The same is true for our reality - we only see until the horizon, and we don't believe that there can be anything hidden from our sight beyond what we can see. But there is much more than we'd ever expected. However, to discover what is waiting for us beyond our horizon, we need to approach the background. Instead of merely reaching the horizon, we will get to know what is waiting for us beyond it.

We never know what is beyond our horizon, and thus, we don't realise many options that exist. We can never be sure that something we wish for is impossible.

How can we make our wish more likely?

And how do we know what direction we need to move towards the horizon to make our wish's fulfilment more likely?

Of course, we need to move somewhere, and the best way would be in the direction that brings us into contact with our wish, be it through people who know about it, through a hobby, through a project, or whatever is possible right now. If we move, we can approach the horizon, and we will discover a new territory of possibilities beyond the old horizon.

Knowing what you want

At the same time, it is very beneficial to know precisely what you are looking for and to keep your eyes open! You'll discover more opportunities and possibilities that might lead you to the attainment of your goal if you determine exactly what you are looking for. Ask yourself what the optimal outcome would be. Then keep it in your mind, and check for opportunities wherever you are.

On your way to making a wish possible, remember to:

- Move towards your horizon to discover the unknown.
- Determine what you are looking for accurately, and keep your eyes open for it.

Then you might be the one to prove that the assumed impossible is indeed possible.

One last word about "Nothing Is Impossible": You might find that there are goals that you cannot realise. However, that 96% of our wishes that we assume to be impossible ARE POSSIBLE because even the word impossible says I'm possible. And therefore, it is worth giving your dreams a try.

Anyone can achieve anything. Nothing is impossible. You just have to decide that it IS possible and that you will do it. Impossible should not be found in your dictionary, replace that word with the word "hard".

Anyone that can imagine his or her dream can also accomplish it. You can make anything happen.

The first step is, in fact, imagining your dreams coming true. When you are certain in your mind that you will reach your goal, then you are already halfway there.

Chapter 3

Mind power

What is mind power?

Mind Power is the power or ability of the mind to achieve our desires. Fulfilling desires is only one of the powers. There are a lot of powers of mind to do different things. Some of them are, with the help of your account, you can have psychic powers, you can develop your intuition, also you can move objects, which is called telekinesis, you can develop telepathy, change your behaviour, change your habits, etc.

It is believed that regular persons use only 3 percent of their mind and great scientists use 5 percent of their minds. So, imagine how a person could be if he uses at least 10 percent of their mind.

The essential practice to achieve these mind powers is to calm your mind, which could be obtained by practising meditation. Even practising meditation is not so easy as it is challenging to ease our mind. But, if you practice every day for few moments, you can achieve within few days or maybe months. There are a lot of resources and e-books available online to improve your meditation techniques.

Meditation is not necessary for improving your mind power, but it helps to acquire powers easily and quickly. The most effective mind power is a power of imagination also called the power of visualisation.

Power of Imagination is nothing but the power of your looking with your mind's eye. It means you can achieve your goals whatever you imagine or visualise in your mind. You have to believe every day whenever you get time to reach your goals. But you can ask why everyone cannot achieve their goals? The answer is, everyone can imagine what they desire, after visualisation completed, they again think negatively and have negative beliefs. That's the reason, most of the people cannot achieve what they want. So, when you are imagining, always think positive and believe that you can get what you want. Even, prayers will be answered in the same way. You have to understand what you pray for, to get them answered.

Your thoughts also have power. Your thoughts accompanied with your emotions make you reach your goals. It is advisable to think always positive even in adverse conditions. Your positive thinking makes you get better ideas and better ways to solve all your problems. With the help of positive thinking and positive affirmations, you can achieve your goals, and even you can change your behaviour. People use positive thinking and affirmations mostly to improve themselves and change their habits like smoking, drinking, improve self-esteem, etc.

There are a lot of other aspects of your mind to achieve what you desire.

Your mind power is your destiny

The human mind power is probably the most significant mystery in the history of humanity.

Despite having gone through thousands of years of civilisations, man has only recently found out that the human brain power is under-utilized. We have travelled so far as to reach the moon, yet most people today have been able to utilise only up to 10 percent of what the brain is capable of achieving.

It holds an enormous power of creation in the universe, yet it is so elusive to many people, who are ever in search of the power that can bring success and glory in life.

From a young age, we learned directly or indirectly what are the essential things we need to do in our life to get ahead in the world. In school, we are taught to study hard to get a proper paper qualification. In work, we know our life single most important purpose is to work hard, continually upgrade our skill sets to stay relevant to the fast-changing world, and to network diligently to widen the power of our social system.

There is always an endless list of things waiting to be accomplished. But sadly, most people never honestly feel secure no matter how hard they have worked. No matter how far people have gone in their pursuit of power, they will inevitably experience an increasing sense of lagging behind, which continuously drain their energy and confidence.

Ironically, the very power that they set out to a pursuit through the acquisition of wealth and status has eventually created a desperate sense of powerlessness deep inside their heart.

Why is it so?

The truth is, in the pursuit of all the powers that should supposedly help us achieve wealth, status and success, people have abandoned the only power that matters in their life, that is, the subconscious mind power.

The subconscious mind power is our innate gift. Not everybody is aware of its potential or even its existence. Some people have probably heard of such inherent power but refuse to believe that it works. Many are aware and thought about this innate power, are learning how to master the technique of tapping the power residing in their subconscious mind.

Our subconscious mind holds power to create anything that our mind can conceive. The very challenge that people face in harnessing their subconscious mind power is how to tame their conscious mind. An account that is untamed wonders in all direction from one moment to another.

A mind with wondering unfocused thoughts has very little power to command the subconscious mind. Just as the laser beam will not have any power when it is scattered.

However, this is precisely the kind of mental state most people have today, as a result of many bombardments of information, stress and temptations in our modern world.

Calming the mind and be still is not the natural state of being for most people. It takes efforts and practices to be able to quiet our conscious mind to control our subconscious mind. Meditation is one right way to tame the mind, but it is by no means a natural process. Some people spend years to perfect their skill of meditation and achieve a state of being unsurpassed before.

Today, studies of the science of mind have provided substantial proofs to confirm the viability of such subconscious mind power; more people are convinced and curious to learn more about how to master their subconscious mind.

The scientific findings on the potential of the human mind are known to be the most significant discovery of our time, with the potential to leapfrogged the progress of our civilisation like the invention of light-bulk, the car, aeroplane, the telephone, etc.

Today, after years of efforts in mind research and brain development, mind tools such as mind hypnosis are available to help people achieve adequate control of their mind. Having a robust memory is like having the anchor for our body, mind and soul, which ensures that every other aspect of life, such as health, mental, emotional, finance, and relationship, will be firmly secured.

Learning how to tap the subconscious mind power is the ultimate life skill anyone should seek to master. It is considered to be knowledge of the highest order, which probably surpasses any other skills in its ability to shape our future and create our life success.

The famous metaphysical scientist and writer, Christian Larson said:

"He who can change his mind every day and think the new about everything every day, will always be well; he will always have happiness; he will always be free; his life will always be interesting; he will constantly move forward into the larger, the richer and the better; and whatever is needed for his welfare today, or that he shall surely have abundance."

"A man may live the way he wants to live when he learns to think what he wants to think."

A balanced body for a balanced mind

The mind is a compelling thing. However, most of us never tap into the total power that our minds have. Our minds even have control over our bodies. If we think that something is wrong with our bodies, our minds are strong enough to make that happen. It works the opposite way as well. We can use our minds to will illnesses and pain away if we have developed our mind to that strength.

As strong as the mind is, however, our bodies can also affect the strength of our minds. For instance, when illness starts wearing our bodies down, our bodies begin wearing our brains down as well. Our attitude and outlook on life are altered, just because we are ill.

We can make ourselves sick, just as we can make ourselves well all with the power of our mind. Our bodies can give us a positive outlook, or a negative outlook, based merely on how our bodies feel. The mind and the body work together. When one is 'up' the other is 'up,' and when one is 'down' the other is also 'down.'

Have you ever had a headache that kept you from concentrating on your work? That is a perfect example of the body ruling the mind. Have you ever had the blues and found that you have no energy? That is an example of the spirit governing the body. The mind and the body often fight for control, but they both work best when they are balanced.

The key is to balance the body so that the mind will be balanced as well. The first step to restoring the body is to get rid of all of the toxins. The world we live in is toxic. No matter how clean you are, no matter how clean your home is, or how health conscious you are - you have toxins in your body, and those toxins need to be flushed out on a regular basis.

Getting rid of toxins lays the foundation to develop a balanced body and mind. You also need to cleanse your colon and restore your pH levels to normal. It also aids in getting rid of toxins, as well as rotting fecal matter that resides in the colon. If you are overweight, you need to start reducing that weight immediately. Being overweight keeps the mind and body out of balance.

Look for a formula that takes care of all aspects of mind and body balance and includes vitamins, macro minerals, trace minerals, amino acids, essential fatty acids, and enzymes.

A product in liquid form promotes elimination, improves absorption, and enhances assimilation to cleanse the colon and restore pH levels. Look for something that detoxifies, promotes healing, and nourishes the body, while fortifying the body with the nutrients that are needed to fight disease and illness. It also needs to combat the ill effects of stress, improves vitality, aids in digestion, reduces cravings, improves the glandular system, promotes energy and stamina, slows the aging process, and improves the memory.

An excellent source of antioxidants contains free radical scavengers that reduce the risk of strokes, heart disease, and cancers. It also has anti-inflammatory properties to reduce inflammation and pain associated with arthritis, sports injuries, and inflammatory diseases.

Overall, Body Balancing gives you a sense of well-being because it does indeed balance the body. That sense of well-being is a sign of a well-balanced mind!

6 easy to follow tips to improve mind power

Studies have proven that in order for a particular individual to be considered a master or a genius in a particular field, skill, or craft, he or she must have at the very least dedicated 10, 000 hours to hone this skill, craft, or brand of knowledge that he or she is specializing in. At least 10, 000 hours of regular, consecutive and intensive training, and then, he or she can be considered a genius, a master, a virtuoso.

Practice, practice, practice

Therefore, to improve mind power, what you need to do is to practice, practice, practice. All this practice and training must constantly be done and kept regular for all the hard work to take its effect honestly.

Athletes and dancers are excellent examples of this mindset. They train regularly, maintain a strict diet and regimen. They work out typically, and they have coaches who teach them intensively. Even alone they already have that discipline set into them that is quite impressive. Every little thing that they eat, every activity that they take part in and do, every little something that can affect their bodies and system is strictly monitored. Aside from their strict and regularised training, they also practice, and practice. Such discipline is an excellent example of how athletes and dancers perfect their art and thus can also be applied to how one can improve mind power.

Improve mind power through a healthy diet

It's critical to get the right nutrients into the system for the mind to function at its optimum level

In nutrients, of course, to boost the mind's health, you should eat a healthy and complete diet. It is a given in almost any person who wants to be healthy. If focusing on your brain, the foods that can help your mind are nuts- which are high on choline, delicious food for the brain. You should also add a lot of berries like cranberry, blueberries, etc. which are very good for the brain and keeps the signs of aging from affecting your mind's power. Other foods such as grapes, green leafy vegetables, legumes, and others such as broccoli, cauliflower, are also high for the brain. Among other things foods high in carotene such as carrots also help boost the brain's mind power as well as foods rich in omega 3 fatty acids like tuna and salmon.

Snooze your way to improve mind power

Sleep is one of the best things that a brain needs to replenish itself. Studies have proven that the more hours a person misses that is intended for sleep, the more the brain cells suffer, and thus, memory is also affected. A right requirement of at least 7-9 hours should be allotted to give the conscious mind a time to rest and replenish itself through sleep.

Improve brain power through mental stimulation

Mental stimulation improves brain function and protects against cognitive decline, as does physical exercise.

It would be good to do your crossword puzzles, answer your mathematical equations, or play your Sudoku games first thing in the morning before going off to school or work. While travelling towards school, you can even review your notes, or while commuting towards work, you can try reading the newspaper. Before going to bed, it would be good to keep a good book with you so you can learn yourself to sleep.

Journals and blogging to improve mind power

Another good practice to help keep your mind power is to keep a journal or have a blog. Recording the events that happened to you gives your mind a good exercise not just in memory but even though the act of writing and forming the right words, sentences, phrases, etc., you get to exercise more aspects of your thought processes.

Improve brain power through human interaction

It is good to keep contact with other people because human interaction stimulates your brain cells. Conversations with others will invigorate the brain and provide it with a good workout. Debating topical issues with friends and family is an excellent way of exercising and stimulating the brain and oiling the thought processes.

As you get older, your brain needs more of these practices and mental exercises to keep it in shape longer. Studies have shown that people who continue to practice their hobbies, play music, read books, write journals or keep a blog, paint, or enter dance schools, maintain groups or clubs, and have routines or schedules to follow have less mental aging compared to others.

So to summarise, eat right, sleep right, stay positive and stay open and friendly to human interaction, and of course, practice, practice, practice will go a long way to ensure you improve mind power.

Harnessing the power of the mind will bring immense success and happiness in your life.

How to differentiate fear from intuition

What is intuition?

Intuition is the ability to get a sense, understanding, or feeling about something. Your intuition is an aspect of you, and it is an extension of you. It is how you speak to yourself about getting yourself together and making new choices that move you forward into advantageous possibilities. Your intuition can help you see when you are staying in your balance, or if you are getting pulled out of your balance by other people or events.

It has been said that intuition is your voice of higher consciousness, or your divine spirit talking to you. Hunch is not from the logical mind, but from a higher perspective. Albert Einstein once said, "The intellect has little to do on the road to discovery. There comes a leap in consciousness, call it intuition or what you will, the solution comes to you, and you don't know how or why. The precious thing is intuition."

Intuition is defined as immediate insight or understanding without conscious reasoning. When we, as people begin the process of learning to listen to and heed our intuition, we often hit several roadblocks along the way. We often receive negative messages from our parents, teachers, or peers at which point we begin to doubt our intuition. Our intuition gets obscured by the fears and beliefs we have erected in front of it. When we lose trust in our intuitive knowledge, we begin to close down that channel of information by ignoring it. The good news is, though we may shut out the messages we receive from the higher self, the more upper self-continues to give them, so it is impossible to lose the ability to be intuitive entirely.

Some of the roadblocks we hit during the process of reawakening to our intuition are individual, some are unanimous, but perhaps the most substantial consistent barrier we face in this process is how to separate our intuition which comes from our true self from our fear which comes from our ego self.

Though there is a big difference between intuition and fear, understanding that difference at the moment can prove to be daunting. Our higher selves (the origin of intuition) will not interfere with the experience and free will of our separate physical bodies. It is a choice to heed intuition; it is a choice to even pay attention to it. You must invite intuition. Therefore, fear (which is an emotion that belongs to the physical dimension) easily overrides and obscures intuition.

The process of separating fear from intuition can also be a daunting one because it requires that we become intimately acquainted with our fears. We must discover them, be honest with ourselves about them, learn to recognise them, address them and learn to dissolve them. Only then can we discuss what our intuition is telling us. There are many techniques which can be employed to address and dissipate our fears, by doing this; their influences no longer control our lives. But to separate fear from intuition, you must first become acquainted with what your separate worries feel like so that you can identify them when they come up as if they were emotional "flags". You can begin to do this by writing a list of your fears. List every one of your fears that you can think of and keep the list in an easy to access place. When you come across a situation in which you are feeling intense negative emotion, instead of acting on anything, pull out the list and scan it and ask yourself if any of the fears on the list could be creating the sensation. It is an inevitability that you will continue to uncover hidden fears as you advance in your spiritual journey, at which point you can add new ones to the list. If you find one which you think could be causing the sensation, sit in that sensation for a while, becoming intimately aware of its intricacies. Make a study of it. Learn the sensation of that fear. This way, you will begin to recognise those individual fears so that when they come up, you can know that they are not intuition. Intuition comes with a feeling of correctness and affirmation. Intuition will come as a sudden knowing, a gut feeling, though, image, emotion, or bodily sensation. It will be a quiet, clear and often quick impression. Even if the message of intuition is about something negative, it will come across as being delivered in a "neutral" tone.

We will only experience intense emotion with regards to intuition when we begin to feed the intuition with negative thoughts and feed it with fear. Fear is a highly emotionally charged sensation. It conveys no feeling of correctness and no affirmation until you logically talk your way into it. Fear reflects the past (past issues and past psychological pain). Perspective is not possible from a state of fear, it is so strong it is almost blinding and delusional, and there will be no compassionate or transcendental element to it. False guidance is always rooted in fear. It is false guidance because it comes from the inaccurate assumption that the world is unsafe and that you are not secure, so the guidance you will receive will not be aimed at creating and maintaining freedom, abundance, joy and true self-expression. Instead, it will be aimed at increasing your degree of control. Genuine intuitive guidance comes from a place of love and the knowledge that you are safe and secure as you are. If strong negative emotion is involved, you should always be suspicious that you are either dealing solely with fear or that you have clouded an intuition with fear. If, for example, you have a sudden, persistent and robust emotional feeling that something bad is going to happen to someone you love... a fear such as the fear of loss is most likely what you are dealing instead of an actual intuitive insight which is informing you of something which is impending.

The problem with fear is that it is very persuasive. When we do not uncover it for what it is early on, it catches us in a creation trap. The trap is that once a person gets themselves into a state where they convince themselves based on the feeling of fear that something terrible will happen, they often activate a strong enough vibration that they begin to create (by attraction) the negative event. At which point, when it happens they often say... "See... I knew my intuition was right when it said this was going to happen" when it was an event which was created based on a fear (which they mistook for intuition) that made them begin to think negative thoughts with enough frequency that it organised the very event they feared.

If you find yourself in a place where you have uncovered a fear which is clouding intuition, the best way to get back into the state of receptivity to intuition is to meditate or centre the mind. Quieting the mind when it is alive with fear can be difficult, but it is necessary to clear away the mental clutter so that you can access your inner knowing. Begin by using deep diaphragmatic breathing. It will trigger a relaxation response within the body. Close your eyes, and begin to focus on your breathing. If your mind drifts, without getting frustrated that it has wandered; only bring it back to your breath. Do this for as long as it takes for the fear and negative thoughts to fall away leaving behind a quiet, peaceful, centred feeling. Sometimes it helps people to listen to music which reduces this calm, centred state within them. If you find that it is primarily hard to concentrate, it can be beneficial to listen to a guided meditation. Once you are centred for a while in that neutral, peaceful state, you have opened yourself to the flow of intuitive information, and you can pose your question or ask for intuitive guidance. Once you have posed your question, put forth the intention that you will receive your answer and listen. To truly listen for intuition means to listen with all of your senses. Intuitive messages come in many ways, and they come differently to different people. You may hear the answer or see the answer. You may just "know" the answer. You may get a physical sensation such as a chill or hot flash or feel the answer emotionally. As you practice listening and honouring your intuition, you will get better at recognising the ways by which you receive intuitive information no matter what form it may appear in.

There may be times when you are looking for intuitive guidance that you will not receive a clear answer right away; however, the information may come to you later through other synchronised events or possibly through dreams or in future meditations. If you become frustrated and try to force an answer to come, you will block the flow of intuitive information. Just trust that if it is a message your higher self-wants you to know, it will be made known to you, and if you are on the lookout for it, just at the right time, you will see it. You will recognise it right away. Intuitive messages which are ignored merely get louder and louder in their manifestations until they can no longer be ignored.

If it is indeed your goal to become intuitive, you will eventually learn to distinguish the voice of ego from the voice of the true self. Your ego which is driven by fear rationalises as well as creates reasons why you should not follow the instruction of intuition. The truth however, does not need the rational justification that fear needs to be valid. The truth will merely be conveyed over and over again in the same loving, unconditional way until it is received. We must just remember that right intuitive messages are always in the service of our best interests, it is impossible to cut one's self off from the capability of being intuitive, and it is possible to differentiate our fears from the intuitive messages we are receiving every day. All we need is a little practice.

Eight ways your intuition talks to you

Your intuition communicates to you every day. Intuition is your natural ability to sense the truth about people, places, things, and situations, without using logic, physical senses, or prior knowledge. While you're awake and asleep, you receive intuitive messages. Whether you're at home or out in the world, you receive intuitive messages. Your intuition talks to you in eight ways:

1. Intuitive seeing is the ability to see visions and dreams showing images that flash like a camera snapshot, pause like a freeze frame, or roll like a motion picture "out in space" or in your mind's eye. For example, you intuitively see a flashing vision show an umbrella or a raincoat to carry with you despite a sunny forecast from local meteorologists.
2. Intuitive feeling is the ability to perceive information via diverse feelings or sensations within your body. This happens with or without you touching external stimuli, a physical agent provoking an interest or a reaction. For example, you intuitively feel a sudden urge to stop in a convenience store to buy a bottle of water. You run into an old friend you haven't seen in years.
3. Intuitive hearing is the ability to hear various sounds "out in space" or in your head (temporal lobes), throat (inner ear), or heart. For example, you ponder a problem while driving to work and intuitively hear a comedic phrase that helps you solve it.
4. Intuitive knowing is the ability to know information without knowing how and without a doubt. Information pops into the top of your head "out of the blue." For example, you intuitively know an afternoon business meeting will result in an exclusive deal with a new client.
5. Intuitive tasting is the ability to taste various substances without putting anything in your mouth. For example, you intuitively taste sweet honesty or sour dishonesty when questioning your spouse's politics.
6. Intuitive smelling is the ability to smell various scents "out in space" or in your inner nose. For example, you intuitively smell

green vegetables to eat for dinner, though you seldom buy them from a farmer's market or grocery store.
7. Intuitive speaking is the ability to speak abrupt, insightful sayings to others and yourself without thinking what to say. For example, you intuitively speak about a natural disaster affecting a country and it happens the next day.
8. Intuitive singing is the ability to sing sudden, edifying songs to others and yourself without hearing external music. For example, you run errands and intuitively sing Arrested Development's song "Tennessee." Then you find out that your next family reunion will be held in Nashville, TN.

When you receive an intuitive message, it's important to be aware of it in progress. Then trust your intuition and act on its guidance. You receive validation instantly or later. The "point of no return" comes when it's too late to act on an intuitive message, no matter the situation. It plays out for better or worse. Your intuition helps you in twenty-eight areas of life, including career, finances, health, and relationships. Stay in the intuitive flow and be blessed.

8 ways to sharpen your intuition and make your life better

Even if you have not been accustomed to listening to your intuition, or trusting your intuition, you have this fantastic power! Read below for the eight best strategies to help you hone your intuitive abilities to assist you in making better decisions for your life.

Self love

Intuition is not something outside of yourself. It is not someone else telling you what to do. Hunch is your own higher perspective. You desire to express yourself creatively in all that you do. Your intuition is your infinite capacity to search for and find, creative solutions for your challenges and your life. Most everyone already knows that when you ignore intuition, the situation does not turn out so well. Allowing yourself to invite more of your intuition into your life is a powerful act of self-love. By embracing your intuition, you show compassion for yourself and choose to bring more positive outcomes to your life.

Listen to your body

Intuition is accurate information from your spirit. Your intuitive messages can come in some forms. You may hear actual words, see a clear image, or have a deep inner knowingness. Your intuition may communicate with you in the way of hunches, insights, Aha! Moments, a feeling, a sixth sense, or various types of body sensations. You may also experience intuition by noticing synchronicities. Set your intention to see the many individual ways your intuition communicates with you.

Embrace quietness

Intuition is initially often a quiet, gentle nudge. It does not shout loud enough to be heard over your stress, upset, frustration, anger, or judgement. Spending some quiet, contemplative time each day is an excellent way to strengthen your intuitive voice. Only sit in a quiet place every day for about 1 to 20 minutes. Take a deep breath, and ask, "What is it I need to know?" or, "What will move me one step closer to a more fulfilling and meaningful life. Then be open. Release your need to think, analyse, and know everything. The best information comes from the quiet guidance of your intuition.

Sit with your problem

Try this experiment. When something is genuinely troubling you, just sit with it. Don't do anything to fix or solve the problem logically. Instead, just relax, place your intention on allowing the best possible outcome, and breathe. See if you can step away from the negative thoughts circling with frenzy within your head. Your intuition sees many creative ways to bring about a goal or bring about a positive outcome to your situation. Your job is to stop fretting and stressing with the problem, and instead, place your focus on being open to amazing new potentials. Decide to allow your intuition to get involved in your life.

Play games with your intuition

Play fun little games with yourself that allows intuition to expand. For example, when standing in front of a bank of elevators, ask your intuition to "tell" you which elevator will reach your floor first. If you guess correctly, make a big deal of it. Let your intuition know it did a great job and how happy you are to hear from it. Notice how good you feel and breathe into that feeling. Let yourself know that you want more of this type of intuition that feels good. It doesn't matter if your correct guess was just a fluke or intuition. Your purpose is not to second guess, but to build up more of what you want. If you guessed incorrectly, just shrug it off. Let your intuition know that you may have ignored it in the past, but you are now ready to begin listening and taking action on its wisdom. Have some patience with yourself. Once you decide that you want more intuitive information in your life, it will begin showing up. Allow yourself to turn those little initial successes into avenues of greater intuition.

Ask intuition based questions

Questioning is one of the best ways to develop stronger intuition and gain clarity and insight. When getting in touch with your intuitive self, ask questions that would lead you forward into positive solutions. Ask formed questions that allow clear answers. For example, you might ask, "What is the next step I could take that would bring new energy and new passion?" Intuition can bring you down paths you hadn't considered. Intuition can show you new ways to try and new possibilities. Your intuition is infinitely inventive. When listening for your intuitive answers, remember that you may get your answers from a variety of sources including hunches, coincidences, feelings, words, or even physical sensations.

Follow your intuitive hunches

Once you get an intuitive idea, decide to take action. It doesn't have to be a huge life-changing action, but you can take one small, comfortable step in the direction of your intuitive guidance. On a day-to-day basis, allow your intuition to play a more significant role in your life. If you have the sense to take a left turn instead of a right turn, follow through and go left. If you are grocery shopping and the broccoli somehow calls to you instead of the carrots you had intended to purchase, buy the broccoli. You don't need to logically question "why" you turned left or bought broccoli. Your goal is to create a bond of trust between your logical self and your intuitive self. When you fail to follow your hunches and gut feelings, talk to your intuition. Tell it that it did an excellent job of providing useful information. Let it know that yes, it would have been wise to follow through with the natural course of action, but this time you choose not to. However, let your intuition know that you still want the input even though you might not always listen.

Journal

Writing is a gateway to the soul which means it is also a gateway to your intuition. Exploring with pen and paper allows a process to unfold of reconnecting with hidden aspects of your self. It helps you speak out, allowing ideas to become actual words. It will enable vague concepts to take shape in the safety of a journal. Writing is a powerful tool that allows what is often locked away inside to have access to the world. It allows you to feel into your physical body and connect with intuition, creativity, and imagination. Writing allows the time to find precisely the right words or the most powerful images to express your self. It takes fuzzy or confusing images and brings them into sharp focus. Writing is an easy way to gain insight from your intuition.

Intuition is your higher perspective and guidance. Since it is an aspect of you, it holds your best interests for creating a fulfilling and meaningful life. Hunch is your urge to creatively manifest your most fulfilling and meaningful life, your goals, your dreams, and all that is good and beautiful. Utilize these eight suggestions to sharpen your intuition, and you will be surprised at how often it will give you a shortcut to the life and outcomes you want.

Chapter 4

Detachment the key to getting what you desire

Emotions. We all have them. They can cover a wide range. We can choose to hide them or express them. But the most important thing you can do is detach from them if you want to achieve what we desire.

To successfully attract something, you must be detached to the outcome. If you are attached to the result of something you desire, you project the negative emotions of panic, disbelief, distrust, pessimism, fear or yearning which attracts the opposite of your goal. When you expect these negative emotions, you are functioning from a position of fear, anxiety, and doubt instead of confidence, trust, belief, trust and peace.

Attachment

What is an attachment? Attachment is being POWERLESS. When you devote all or most of your energy and time to something, you are attached to it. When you look to the external, to outside sources, to complete you, to make you whole, to provide your happiness and fulfilment, you are attached and powerless. You have abandoned your reference, your core, your self. You have enslaved you to the situation or another person.

Attachment creates insecurity. You spend your time worrying if you will get what you want and if you get some of it you worry about how you will maintain it and whether you will lose it. Attachment occurs when we demand that everything is known to us. It is an attachment to the known. We request, fret and get angry over not knowing how something will be achieved. We lack trust and have no faith. Accessory sets you up for days and nights of crying, worrying, raging, feeling jealous, overeating and feeling sorry for yourself.

Detachment

What is detachment?

Detachment is being POWERFUL. It is when you let go and let nature (or the Universe or whatever you want to call it). It is when you step back and decide that whatever the outcome and the journey to that outcome you will grow, learn and in the end, have something good. Yes, you may get exactly what you want or no, you may not, but instead, you will get something entirely satisfying. Detachment is deciding that either way, you will be pleased with the outcome.

Have you noticed that sometimes the harder you try to work out something the worse the situation gets? That is when you are being told to detach. When you use force, you create new problems. When you allow God/the Universe to work, achievement is effortless. The best thing for you to do is to take control when and where you can and when you meet the wall of resistance that tells you to release - release!! The situation will work out, and you can sit back and reap the fruits/profits etc.

Being detached permits you to change your focus and shift to something new if necessary. It means you can go with the flow, without giving up on your intention.

You do not need a rigid, inflexible, detailed plan laid before about how you will get what you want. When you surf the waves of the unknown and let uncertainty wash around you, you become flexible, spontaneous and open to a wide range of opportunities that can be blessings to you. You have experiences you might not have had otherwise and meet people you would not have otherwise encountered.

Detachment means realising that the Universe is delivering good things to you and doing good things through other persons and you. It means realizing there is nothing you need to force. It's all good. With this in mind, do you realise you can have anything through detachment? A home. A car. A mate. A job.

Embrace your desire and intentions but do not cling to them. State your intentions and desires and rest knowing they will be accomplished.

The Law of Attraction tells us that what we experience is a result of what we feel; it is a result of our attitude. If we are detached from the outcome, feeling calm and know that the issue will be a good one, we will get a good outcome. You may not get the specific job or boyfriend you wanted, but you will get a fantastic job or a boyfriend who loves you so profoundly you, and you him, that you cannot imagine life without him!

Remember, whatever you detach from has no power over you, preferably you have absolute control over it.

For example, if you desire a loving and intimate relationship with a particular man who makes himself emotionally and physically unavailable, right now, detach. State your intention and desire to have a loving, intimate relationship with this man, but detach knowing that you will either get a loving and close relationship with this man or he will be replaced with someone beautiful who will make you forget all about this emotionally unavailable man. In that case, that unavailable man is the loser in this situation if he does not awaken and see your value; you are have lost nothing of value if he does not!

Along the journey, you can be open and flexible enough to learn about yourself and why you were attracted to an emotionally unavailable man. See? You grow emotionally and spiritually, and you get a great relationship - all by practising detachment. Achieve your intentions from a position of power. Detach and let it all work out. It's all good!

Get what you want

Are you mostly fearful or mostly secure? Is your belief in lack and scarcity and "hard times" stronger than your opinion in ease, joy and abundance? When you focus on fear, you will create plenty of fearful things to fret about. If on the other hand, you focus on joy and laughter, you will attract plenty of fun and funny things in your life.

Perhaps it is seen as childish in today's severe life to not worry about the world's problems? Maybe it is seen as uncaring or cold not to worry about other people's problems. It is damaging to you to focus on anything other than joy. That may be a dramatic statement to make, but it's true. You own happiness is at stake every time you focus your attention on anything other than feeling happy.

Feeling joyous should not be a rare experience we only experience some of the time. It should be the norm. Beautiful things should not just happen to "other people" they should happen to us a lot. And these joyous moments can happen to us all the time if we allow them to. All we have to do is try our best to focus on joy every moment we can remember.

A lot of people look at what their lives lack and then determine that lack to be the problem. They see a lack of positive things happening to them and therefore think that if more positive things happened to them, then life would be so much better.

This format of "looking at lack" is most prevalent in financial categories. People see a lack of finances and believe that lack of money is the problem. They say things like, "If I had more money; if I was out of debt; if I could just earn more money..." They then conclude, "Not having enough money is the problem in my life."

What so many fail to realise is that lack is not the problem. Lack of your life is never the problem! Lack is merely the effect of something going on inside the mind.

You are indeed free to focus on your lack and just accept it. That is a possible mindset, and that's your privilege. You can focus on all your limitations and excuses and just take that. That is also a mindset. You have free will to that if you want to.

A better choice is to focus your mental attention on your desires and destinations in life. You can picture in your mind who you desire to be and where you desire to go. That too is a mindset. You have the free will to think that way if you choose to.

What you focus your mind on is what you will bring into your life. It is a tried and true principle of life that works just like the law of gravity. If there is a lack in your life, then refuse to focus on that lack and refuse to accept that lack. Instead, make a conscious decision to start focusing on your desired destination.

Goal setting-how to get what you want

The process of getting what you want is a simple, goal achievement plan that a lot of people just do not take seriously. They go on day after day, not knowing what they want or how to go about getting it. If you have set goals for yourself and wanted to ensure that you achieve them, let me show you a very only method of taking one specific purpose and using it as the means of getting what you want. Here is how the process works:

Select a goal

We all have a few goals that we would like to achieve. In this process, select a target that is the most important to you right now, the one that will bring you the most satisfaction. It could be, starting a business, earning a specific amount of money, learning a new skill, and so on. Write the goal down on a piece of paper, or better yet, on a large whiteboard so that you see it every day.

Put a time on it

Choose a date of completion for this goal. A goal without a specific date attached to it is only a wish. Be realistic in setting the date of termination. Wanting to earn a million dollars in the next twelve months is not as likely as wanting to receive one hundred thousand dollars in that same about of time. It must be in your time frame, not someone else.

Amount of money needed

How much money will you need to get what you want? Is it five thousand or ten thousand per month? How many sales would you have to make to get this money? Break it down per day and month. How many leads and phone calls would you have to make to get the sales? Break it down per day and month. You must stay focused in this part of the process.

Time investment

There will have to be a certain amount of time invested in talking to prospects or clients, acquiring new skills (as needed), and working on yourself (personal development). It will require discipline, persistence, and consistency throughout the process. Record your progress and celebrate those small victories. If you want to get what you want, it will take work. No one said it would be easy, but with hard work and discipline, the experience will be a well worth ride. Utilize the process described, stay focused, keep your mindset right, and visualise getting what you want daily until you have it. It is yours for the taking, get it.

7 secrets of using what you've got to get what you want

Start slow take baby steps

The most prominent single factor that keeps otherwise successful people from reaching their goals is their unwillingness to start small. As a result, the mistakes they make have more of a tendency to overwhelm them, causing them to abandon their goal. Start slow, give your confidence a chance to grow. As your confidence builds, your self-motivational energy toward the project will increase also.

Persistence

Another word for persistence is "keep-trying ness or never quitting easy. A persistent attitude is a trait that can be developed, just as a weightlifter can strengthen a muscle, or a runner can develop endurance by running. Persistence can be generated by refusing to quit at the first signs of defeat or opposition. With each victory, you achieve you will develop the attitude of perseverance.

Assertive self starter

Be alert to opportunities to take action toward your goals, however.

Small. Just start where you stand. Be Observant - Don't just look at things, see them, see the details. That's often the difference between the amateur and the professional. The professional can see the details of a problem the rookie can't. Because of this ability to observe more of the features, society gives the respect, money and many other rewards to the professional.

Present mindedness

Most procrastinators find it challenging to think in the present. The procrastinators (and worriers) think future tense. They think "what could happen if?" The self-starter feels in the present. The self-starter thinks in the now? For honestly, that's all we have. As the saying goes, yesterday is gone and tomorrow is not here yet. All we have is now to do good, to improve our world or help others.

Independence

The self-starters make up their minds after the fact are known. They can't afford to wait or depend on the opinion of others to do their thinking for them. The definitely can't wait for other to motivate or move them to action.

Ability to fail constructively

It is a vital trait of successful people. They're not afraid to fail. Why? Because they know how to fail. They learn from their failures and try again until they succeed. Low achievers are so scared of failure and thus never work, they lose by default. By striving, success is not guaranteed, but if one doesn't try, failure is guaranteed.

Ability to shake discouragement

The bounce back secret of most people who succeed is this one trait. Contrary to popular belief, it's not just the failures in life who experience discouragement. By reading biographies of the famous and successful, you'll find most had one thing in common. What? They all had obstacles, problems and setbacks along the way that could have caused discouragement. However, they were able to shake melancholy and continue toward their goals until they were achieved.

Manifest what you desire into reality

What are your desires? How would you define desire? Defining passion can be a challenge, given that several definitions fit the word. Desire is a recurring theme in philosophy just as it is a topic of debate in psychoanalysis. Desire represents wanting in economics and greed in some concepts of morality. It is commonly associated with interpersonal attraction, as well as sexual libido, whether rational or given to an intense "lust" for gratification. However, when the discussion centres on desire in an everyday context it usually refers to human motivation, which is a thought that leads to action. Motivation is not something lustful or unnatural. Every human being desires. Every man and woman wants something greater than temporary gratification.

Defining what specifically that desire can be more complicated. Different people want different things, based on numerous factors such as their personality, their background, their circumstances and their genetic disposition. Some people desire money and a higher lifestyle. Other people have no great desire for material wealth but want to make a difference on a large scale. Other people are motivated by art and have a message to share with others.

There is no one truth when it comes to labelling human desire, as in one thing that every man wants. Some needs must be fulfilled. There is a need for recognition, whether that comes from individuals, organisations or invisible entities. There is a need for interpersonal relationships, as no man is an island, and does require the company of others to feel complete. However, it would be inaccurate to suggest that every person desires money, fame and power. Even if those achievements were high on a person's priority list, one could not assume that every wealthy, famous person is a selfish being at heart. Some entrepreneurs worth billions of dollars made their mark in history by donating large sums of money to charity. On the other hand, it cannot it be assumed that a person who intentionally seeks a life of poverty is genuinely humble or giving.

Desire merely is what drives us as human beings, however noble or vain those intentions are. It is what we want and what we yearn for. In determining what your desires are, it's important to ask yourself why you want these things. Many people today have their desires programmed, and only want what the media implies is the American dream. Television, Internet, movies and books may idolise beauty, wealth and instant gratification. Ask yourself challenging questions like, would you want money if it had no monetary value and didn't "buy" you anything? If you did have great wealth and had already taken care of your immediate needs, what else would you do with your resources? What is your attitude regarding interpersonal relationships, love, family and children? How do you feel about the current political climate and various environmental issues?

Ultimately, desire is so much more than just satisfying strong temporal urges related to hunger, sex, love and aesthetics. The human mind experiences both conscious and unconscious thought. Man is also the only animal capable of existential theory, and many believe, the only animal capable of a more profound sense of spirituality. Though contemporary society may judge the value of a person on their net worth, many of the wealthiest people throughout history have sought greater understanding than just the pursuit of wealth. The happiest people in life are not the ones that lose sleep over business matters 24 hours a day. Preferably, they are the ones that enjoy life to its fullest, regardless of what they have. They take in all of life's priceless moments. For the pleased person, money is a reward, or a byproduct-success is all about personal achievement.

Many people have a philanthropic desire. One way to be able to donate even more money, time, and expertise is to realise your goals in the timeframe you desire so you can begin implementing your philanthropic desires, maybe even sooner than originally planned.

It's very understandable that you want many good things in life, both temporal and internal treasures. However, to get what you desire, to achieve your highest ambitions, you must reach out and make that effort. It will require you to focus on the details and to create a workable plan. You will set realistic goals for yourself and work hard to achieve those goals. You will not view a challenge as a crushing defeat or a setback as a complete failure. If you have indeed committed yourself to your vision of success, then you are already living your dream. All the financial rewards and high respect that accompany your achievement is just secondary.

Manifest desires get what you want

Many people may think that it is not easy to manifest desires. But let me tell you a secret: it is easy to do that. The first step is essential. Once you can make that one step to manifest desires, well then everything else will be easy. To manifest desires, it is imperative that you practice meditation on a regular basis.

The law of attraction must work to manifest desires. It is here that you must want something hard and want it the right way and then the forces of the universe will work so that you will get what it is that you want. It may be success, wealth, inner peace, or romance. Needing them is not enough though. You have to know the reason why you want them. In that way, you fuel the fire and keep it burning.

Here are some helpful things that you may be able to use to manifest desires. First of all, look into your emotions and sense the feeling of having that particular thing that you want. How do you feel? Let us say that you desire success in work. If you see yourself successful, that is great? You will be praised, and people will look up to you, and there is that expected hike in salary. Let yourself feel the yearning to live that dream. You are then starting to add more energy to your desire. See yourself looking at your new check, sitting in your new office.

Imagine what everything looks, feels and smells like. Imagine the feeling you have of loving the work your doing, looking up at the clock and smiling.

Now that you sense the feelings of having your desires add a picture to it. Visualize yourself being successful. See yourself being able to do more with the success that you have achieved. Are you having fun?

Now you must believe that you can, and you will manifest desires of your heart. That faith that you have will create a connection to the universe and through Divine Intelligence. Expect to demonstrate the things that you want.

So as long as you believe that you will get what you desire, you will get it.

Chapter 5
Ask, believe, receive

It almost sounds too simple! All I have to do is ask, then believe I'll receive it! The toughest part of the three for many is not being prepared to accept.

The truth is, most of us don't ask, most are too distracted to focus on believing for very long, and finally, even fewer are truly prepared to receive. Asking Believing and Receiving is a process that has been proven to work time and time again.

Many people are disappointed with their lives because they don't get what they think they deserve. They tend to believe that it will all be brought to them without asking. That is just plain wrong. No one can read your mind. You have to ask to receive something. Here are some steps and useful tips:

Create a picture of what you want

But before you ask, you have to know what exactly you want to receive! It is something that most people overlook when they aren't satisfied with current situation. They know that they need some change, but they don't know what exactly they want. To pull out good results, you can say that you disapprove current situation - but you have to support your statement with your opinions, wishes and needs. Take your time and think about your needs. Create a clear picture of that and then proceed with changes. As we all know, no matter how bad situation is, change doesn't have to be positive.

Express your needs

When you talk about what you want, don't hesitate. Say it openly; "I want this, this and that!". Problems with a lot of people are that they believe they've expressed themselves, while in reality they only said hints. And then even if others want to help you, they can't because they don't know what exactly you want. Another important thing is to speak of using "I statements". That way you give your words more significant meaning and increased importance.

Pick right time for conversation

Even though almost every moment can be useful for starting that kind of conversation, some moments should be avoided. For example, you shouldn't express your wishes shortly or during arguments or fights. That might give a different light to your opinions. You have to find perfect moment for expressing your feelings and needs.

Here's how to ask, believe & receive

1. **The attitude of gratitude**: You always notice others when they are incredibly grateful. Ask yourself, how grateful am I. Grateful for even the smallest of things. You need a Grateful List! Things you are thankful for every day, the most trivial things matter as much as anything else. Let it become your primary attitude. Nothing connects quicker with the Law of Attraction than an Attitude of Gratitude. Gratitude is a reciprocal energy force. It is an important point, and you should write it down, appreciation is a complementary energy force! Simply put, you get back what you give.

2. **Emotional intelligence:** Is about keeping your emotions balanced and void of any ego. Ego is the big disconnect from the energy field we call the Law of Attraction. When your emotional intelligence is engaged you'll notice you are far more tolerant of others, you are a great listener, and seem to have an endless supply of empathy and compassion. On a scale of 1 to 10, how's your EI or emotional intelligence score?

3. **Clarity and focus:** When you make the time and clear away all the daily noise or distractions, it's quite easy to focus on Asking, then Believing and the secret weapon of the three, the real ability to Receive. Most often we are never ready to Receive. "oh no I couldn't accept that" .. ever heard yourself say that? When things are offered or given, accept it willingly, with an attitude of gratitude. Receiving completes the energy transaction, regardless of what the item is. The more often you can Receive, the more your receiving channel is open. When things come your way, they come with energy, receive it openly and willingly always. Ideas will flow to you with greater ease, as you have no barriers put up. The universe wants to give you things every day, be alert and ready to Receive them. It may

seem foreign, but your ability to receive is every bit as important as your willingness to give. They go hand in hand.

4. **Multi-tasking:** ALERT GUYS! It applies to so many things we try to do in a day. Anyone who is in serious multi-tasking mode does themselves a great disservice. No time to be grateful, indeed no time for balanced, clear emotions and least of all, any clarity or focus. Multi-tasking by nature just keeps "fitting things in". Pretty much zero quality there. Asking, Believing and Receiving is a mindset, one that does require some attention to detail, so set some time aside to do it properly.

Five hidden benefits that come from asking to receive

Without stating the obvious, asking for what we need gives us a better chance of receiving than not doing so. Things get a little complicated when other factors cloud our thoughts such as pride, making it difficult for us to seek the help that we need. Asking to can be made a lot easier when we understand the full implications of our actions and the other benefits which this offers that are not so apparent. Below are some of the reasons why it is important to ask to receive.

Humility

Asking others for help means we accept that we are incapable of coping on our own. It doesn't say that we are weak, it just means that we need help. The holy scriptures teach us to ask and believe that we shall receive, if we do so with the right intentions, then we shall get our desires. God does not place us in situations of tribulation without a means of rescue. We just have to be willing to seek this rescue for it to work for us.

Allowing others to receive blessings

The Bible also teaches us that we are more blessed when we give than when we receive. If we are in the habit of giving to others, then we should know that we would always receive blessings. However, there is a balance in all things so we must also allow others to give to us for them to receive blessings as well. If they are in the position to give, then we should let them do so, this way we all recognise our worth and grow spiritually.

Leading by example

The creator teaches us that we are examples for others to learn from and lead their lives. Each of us has something within ourselves that another admires. Our actions are they unimportant to us personally serve a higher purpose to those that respect us. If we show them how to overcome tough situations by the methods revealed to us through scriptures, then they are bound to do the same in turn. Asking to receive is one of those examples that we can teach others of our humility, our faith and the word of the creator.

Helping others help us

Sometimes other people are waiting for us to ask for this help. They do not know how to offer it because we always appear to be self-sufficient. Perhaps this may not be the case in all instances, but we must understand that a burden shared is a burden halved. When we ask for this help, we are giving our helpers the opportunity to support and aid us in the way in which we desire. If we do not ask then the advice we get may not necessarily meet our needs.

The creator can help us through other people

The creator is in us in the truth as he is in others. When we pray to him, he can decide to answer our prayers through others. Sometimes seeking this help is finding the answer to our prayers. We cannot determine what HE thinks before we act. We can only act with good intentions and hope that we are walking in the steps of the Lord. It is only by our faith that we know that God has responded to our prayers even though we had to ask to receive.

Chapter 6
Power of focus

Focus is so dominant it can be used to cut steel

With power as low as 800 Watts, hardly enough to heat the average room, a light source can be focused to form an intense pinpoint of energy less than 1mm in diameter which contains enough energy to cut through sheet steel with high accuracy. It is a beautiful testimony to the power of focus. Scattered energy produces little, if no result, whereas very carefully focused energy will produce surprising results!

What is focus

Dictionary.com defines Focus as a noun describing "a central point, as of attraction, attention, or activity."

Wikipedia defines Focus as related to psychotherapy and related disciples as follows; the term focusing is used to refer to the simple matter of holding a kind of open, non-judging attention to something which is directly experienced but is not yet in words. Focusing can be used to become clear on what one feels or wants. Focusing is set apart from other methods of inner awareness by three qualities: something called the "felt sense", a condition of engaged accepting attention, and a philosophy of what facilitates change.

Focus determines our future.

Tony Robbins can be quoted "What you focus on consistently, you tend to manifest in your life."

Chris Howard can be quoted "Where attention goes, energy flows and results show"

These are 2 compelling quotes, and there are many more, please add yours to the comments area below.

Focus starts in our mind then shows in our behaviour. The focus is not only in our mind it is in our actions. Our mind creates the works that we use to produce our future.

Our brain processes massive amounts of information every moment

Our brain takes in around 2 million sensory inputs in every second in the form of sights, sounds, touch, tastes and smells, of course, that is not our experience though, this is because we cannot process that much information, so our brain uses filters to delete, distort or generalize the sensory input into about 7 internal representations, or "chunks" that our brain can find useful. To reflect this in Neuro-Linguistic Programming (NLP) terms "The Map is not the Territory", in other words, what we see is not a complete representation of-of what is going on around us. That raises the question; What are we missing? Could it be the next fantastic opportunity? Could it be a danger approaching? Could it be how blessed we already are? Could it be the Acres of Diamonds that we have right beneath us?

You get what you focus on

As more eloquently stated by Tony Robbins and Chris Howard in the above quotes, you get what you focus on. Why? Because we have conditioned our brain to delete, distort and generalise.

Imagine are in a dark room with a torch and need to exit the room quickly. If you have been taught to shine the torch at the floor when you use a torch, all you will see is the floor ahead of you, as you walk forward you soon bump into a wall and have no way out. If you have been taught to rapidly wave the torch up and down and around about in random movements, you may see lots of the room, but still may miss finding the door and the window that you could use to exit. Both these example are extremes, yet are more common than you think. How often have you met somebody who proudly states "we have always done it this way"? Or somebody who jumps from one great idea to the next every day? How many of you have seen this behaviour in your own life? I know it has held me back a lot in the past!

Where you shine the "Flashlight of your focus" determines what you "see". We will deal more with the science behind our thoughts and behaviours at another time, for now, let's just think about 2 key points:

If you try to focus everywhere, you scatter your energy and potentially miss the right best opportunity for you.

If you stay focused on the wrong thing, you will get the incorrect results. (it has been said that it is crazy to think that you can keep doing the same thing and get different results)

Let's turn the above points around:

If you place your focus in the right place, you will concentrate your energy and create the results you desire!

Focus as it relates to our mind

It is vital to creating the correct focus in our mind. For example: If you focus on poverty and you with tend to manifest debt, focus on Prosperity, and you will tend to manifest Prosperity. If you concentrate on sickness or disease you will tend to manifest sickness or disease, focus on Health you will tend to manifest Health. If you focus hatred, you will tend to manifest hatred, focus on Love you will tend to manifest Love. If you focus on boredom, you will tend to manifest boredom, and if you concentrate on Fun, you will manage to Manifest Fun. What do you focus on most of the time?

To create the focus of our thoughts here are some things that will assist:

Be aware: Now that you know the effect of focus watch yourself and your results, see the impact that focus has on your life.

Be grateful: Regularly (once a day or more) take account of all the things you are grateful for. If you are having a challenging day and nothing seems to be worth being grateful, push through the mental barriers and ask "If there was something to be grateful for, what would it be". It shifts your mind into a state of looking for the best.

Know your outcome: Steven Covey states "Begin with the end in mind". Take some time to think about what you would like to achieve from life. Break this down into measurable goals that you can use to align your focus with.

Acknowledge everything: It is essential to acknowledge everything that is happening or has happened in the past. All these things affect the "filters" our brain uses to delete, distort or generalise. If your car had faulty brakes and you failed to acknowledge it then it would not matter how much you focused on stopping, it would not stop. There is a lot of theory about the conscious and sub-conscious mind that could be discussed around this topic, however, for now, let's just trust and use this simple process:

Acknowledge all that is so

Make it OK (this may include acceptance of the issue and forgiving yourself and others)

Choose how you would like it to be. It determines your future focus.

Condition our mind for the outcome we desire: Here are some brief suggestions:

Write your goals down,

Read your goals regularly remind yourself of these goals

Use techniques such as "the magnetic goal drop" to place the target into your sub-conscious mind

Use affirmations to tell yourself about the behaviours you need

Take time to pray and meditate on your desired outcome

Focus as it relates to our use of time

Time is said to be the "one true equaliser of all people", we all have 24 hrs in a day, 365 days in a year, no other thing brings the same equality as time. In effect, we choose our use of time from our mind. However, it is useful to look at this separately and address some of the external conditions we need to create to allow us to focus:

Set aside time each day where you can be undisturbed to "clear your mind of the clutter" and make the space to focusing your mind. Catherine Ponder teaches about the "Prosperity law of Vacuum", in summary; For us to place something into our life, we must first have the space vacant for it to fill. Undisturbed time may require the following:

- Turn off the phone

- Turn off the email

- Turn off instant messaging

- Lock your office door or escape to a quiet location

- Let others know you are not available at that time

Set aside time for specific tasks. It is especially important if they are things you have been procrastinating on, set aside the time and get them done! It is also crucial for keeping yourself up to date with relevant jobs.

Count the cost before you commit. Remember the torch example, if we are scattered in our focus, our results will be limited, and we may miss important opportunities. Being 'spread too thin' does not allow anyone to operate at their optimum. Always ask yourself "how important is this task to achieving my goals".

Focus on one thing at a time. It is known to usually be more effective to take one project to completion before starting the next than to have multiple projects on the go at the same time. Jim Collins refers to the Hedgehog Concept to describe how focused people can achieve more significant results than others. The Hedgehog concept compares two animals; a fox, which is very talented and knows many creative ways to get a meal, and the hedgehog, a somewhat dull animal that knows one, and only one, thing. To roll into a spiked ball for protection. The hedgehog always wins, because, despite the fox's many clever tricks and high intelligence, there's no getting around a spiky ball. It highlights how one good solid strategy can be more potent than many "clever" strategies.

Focus: follow one course until successful

Focus Now! You are not indeed focused unless you are present. Your mind and body must be aligned, alert and thinking about what you are doing right now, not what happened yesterday, not what you are going to do next, but what you are FOCUSING on RIGHT NOW!

One of the most compelling reasons why businesses fail, or business owners, managers, and salespeople do not succeed is their lack of keeping a focus on what is vital, relevant, and results-oriented. It is this lack of attention that can bring any well-intentioned business and business owner, manager or salesperson far short of their goal. It can spell the difference between failure and success, moderate income and wealth, obscurity and successful notoriety.

Lack of focus can mean that a home-based business will never get off the ground; the owner/manager will be chasing after every fad or new opportunity rather than digging in and going after the goal. It will mean bursts of start ...and stop; start over again with some new idea ...and stop. It will be like a sailing vessel tossed to and fro by the strong winds and finally capsizing because of the storms. Lack of focus can mean the difference between a substantial online business and continually seek new opportunities where the grass looks greener, never settling in for the long haul. It can mean the failure of a brick and mortar business.

The power of focus is results oriented. Some people centre in on the process but focus centres on the results of the entire project. If you worry about how many phone calls you have to make, or people you need to see, then you will never get off first base and begin to prospect and turn leads into prospects and then into customers.

What is driving you? Do you desire to gain wealth through a successful home-based business or brick and mortar business? Do you wish to be independently wealthy? Are you seeking more time with your family, before everyone grows up? What are the results you desire for your life, your business, your family?

The power of focus says that the results are worth consistency and stick-to-it-ive-ness. Focus does not count the cost (the process) but is determined to pay the price for the achievement of the goal. Focus takes hard work. Focus means remaining on the task when others want to play. Focus does not mean giving up. Focus does not mean jumping after the next great fad. Focus means a 2, 3 and 5 year or more commitment. The power of concentration is most assuredly outcome driven. The result is what is most important (outside of integrity and honesty.)

Outcome driven success is a step by step process. To have a successful business will mean that you have a succession of small wins. You eat the elephant one bite at a time, and you are successful in your business one small victory after another. It does not happen overnight, but day after day after day of little consistent victories and wins can bring a great result.

Often the problem for most people is a focus that is broken. They lose their focus, their drive, their consistent movement toward the one result that they have dreamed and planned and worked for. They get side-tracked and forget what result they want and begin to focus on how to get to that result. You focus when you commit yourself to one goal. You focus when you never quit. You focus when you manage your time so that your commitment is clear. Nothing gets in the way of the goal, time-wise.

The power of focus means that you begin. Too many people never get started. They have the idea. They have the desire. They have the dream. But they never get started. They never leave the starting line, and the thought never happens. The idea never comes to fruition. The business never succeeds. They never risk. They want to play it safe.

The law of attraction and the power of focus

Wonder why people meditate? Wonder why you should always stay calm when things only don't go your way? And wonder why most people cannot perform when under pressure? The reason is simple; you need your mind to focus. You need meditation or any other proven techniques to train your mind in focus. You need to stay calm to concentrate your mind to do things right. You need to get rid of those undesired pressure so as to focus better in performing your task. The power of focus is a significant factor in bring success into your life.

The power of focus is part of your mind power in manifesting your dream into reality. Wouldn't you agree with me that lack of focus is an excellent hinder in pursuing what you want in life? A dream can never be achieved if you do not have the focus on attaining it. When there is no focus, there will be no action and hence, no result. But having said that, how many of us can focus on one goal for an extended period?

Many people can focus for an extended period on the wrong things, that is, focusing on what they do not want in life. And when you keep on focusing on what is not desired, you will get it sooner or later. It is what we refer to as the Law of Attraction. Have you ever wonder why most self-development masters almost always advise you to stop worrying and complaining? Keep focusing on complaining about your job, and you will most likely get more of it. Keep focusing on worrying about your debts, and you will most likely get more of it. Keep focusing on the fear of losing something, and you will most likely lose it one day.

The Law of Attraction is not biased; you do not have to be the selected few to benefit from this law. Anyone who can focus on what he or she wants in life can attain it in the future. If you have heard about this law before but are still quite sceptical, you may like to try it out. After all, there is no harm trying out. However, please focus only on what you want and what is positive. Trying it out by focusing on something negative will undoubtedly get adverse effects. Take one step at a time by focusing on something short term which you can see the result in a day.

Your mind power is a magnetic force, and you attract whatever you put your focus on. That is also why you should train your mind so that you can apply the power of concentration to you. A goal which is not followed by your focus and action, nothing will happen, and your dream will always be just a dream. Be focus and make that enormous difference in your life from today.

Give yourself the gift of time

Have you ever noticed how everyone is in a hurry? People are rushing here and there. People are scurrying to get all the things on their to-do list accomplished by the end of the day only to find that they have another to-do list the next day. Together, moving faster and achieving goals at a faster pace is almost like a national pastime.

Honouring yourself, in many ways, can lead to the new discovery of what makes you the happiest, whether at work, play or in your personal life. Nature has taught us the importance of work and rest and to find a balance between the two. Once you allow yourself the time and space to be in tune with your thoughts, you steadily increase your focus and recharge your energy getting ready to face your world with a fully restored battery.

Taking the time to focus on what's going right in your life is more than just an afterthought; or, at least it should be. The first person that deserves your time, attention and consideration in life should be YOU!

In nature, one of the first things known and maintained for survival is following the ebbs, tides and flow of life; going along with the flow of how things work the best with the least amount of disdain or resistance.

Nature knows when, where and how to take a break. Whether a short quick break, a break to hibernate, a time to honour itself according to the flow of the winds, the tides, the seasons and with good reason; nature always knows exactly when and why to take a break and honour rest and silence.

Like the trees stop growing leaves; hence, they only stop for a short while; their desire is the gift of time to regenerate their energy; replenish their vitality, and honour themselves; take a lesson from the trees and acknowledge yourself as well...

Authorize a block of minutes, make this a daily habit, to give quality time to yourself; be in tune with all the elements that came together and took form in the heavens and manifested on earth; the sole purpose pertaining to you, the perfect designer, knew precisely what to do; with intent, not always seen on the surface; breathing life in you.

You are a three-dimensional being that is the uniquely- unequivocally crafted, gifted, vibrant and uplifted a beautiful human being; THAT"S You, Comprised from the elements; same as the earth's land, water and a bit of salt too; when the creator was done; He took a moment to honor your space; His accomplishment was fun, vibrant and new...

Body; Soul; Spirit, ALL inspired and designed for a unique existence; Aspire to nurture; nourish; encourage; engage in self-knowledge, give back importance to yourself you'll prosper and flourish...

Meditation; exercise; daily prayer, any of these; hopefully, all three; you'll advance your reverie, recovery, or perhaps discovery..

Start with small steps and let your enthusiasm guide you with more time as you extend the process of silent, internal exercise, growing in you a muscle of self-worth, high self-esteem and enjoying your own company throughout the entire process. Get to know yourself as much as you want to get to know others.

Be your own best friend and watch how genuinely engaging you can be to yourself as you relax and reflect in the silent recognition and acceptance of your thoughts and inspired acts that lead to realised dreams, that's if you allow yourself the quiet time to honour yourself!

The first person to receive love from you should be you! Remember to love yourself; honour and appreciate yourself, your time is yours to do as you desire, just don't forget that you are worthy of the silent time to spend in your thoughts.

Learning to take time off is a critical part of your long-term plan for success. Research has shown that those who take a regular vacation are sharper and more productive than those who don't.

Time is eternal

It is in abundant supply, yet, there never seem to be enough of it. Time is precious, but oh, how we squander time on our hands. Time flies, we ask ourselves, where does time go? The clock ticks away and so does our heartbeats as we forge ahead to beat the clock. For some, the 24 hours of a day are not enough to allow them to meet all those commitments that demand time, precious time. People to meet, places to go, things to do and not enough time to do it all!

Thus the word "quality time" has evolved. Do we understand what it means? We share a few minutes or hours with those we love, and we call it quality time. Is this supposed to fill in the large gaps of time away from them? Does this ensure freedom from guilt as we merrily or hurriedly go on from project to project?

Short and sweet takes on a new meaning. At times this is all there is to share. Distance is a great impediment to keeping families in close touch. Celebrations come and go, some family members or close friends will always be absent. They don't have the time to come and share in a ceremony.

But, technology offers a variety of options to keep in touch with anyone, especially those we profess to love. Many of us have forgotten the wonder of the written word- a letter or a card in the mail can bring a smile, tender memories or feelings of joy for the recipient. But who writes letters these days? How much time does it take to call someone just to keep in touch?

Time is a gift many of us forget its value. In the midst of a busy life, it is difficult to find the time to give to anyone but the very immediate family. Even with this limited circle, time can be in very short supply.

Stop a moment and reflect on this. Where and how do we spend our time that justifies the lack of it to share with those we love or care for? The world will not fall apart if you take some time to be with those you love. Your business, your career your hobby, your social life and other commitments that demand part of your time certainly can't take priority over your loved ones.Not all the time.

Time can be budgeted. For those who are too busy to stop and think of where their day goes. How one spends time can be analysed to make more time for the critical issues in life. Remember, years will pass by, lifestyles can change, and health becomes a concern at one point. It can happen to us!

At a particular stage in life, material gifts do not matter. A child would rather have the presence of Mom and Dad at school functions or other activities. It gives that re-assurance that they care. These memories will be cherished for a long time. An expensive gift. Spells guilt and cannot fill in a void nor smooth out feelings of resentment and disappointment.

As we get older, presents do not have the lustre these once had. Tastes and circumstances change. Time becomes a very dominant part of life at this stage. Precious time shared leaves a feeling of being loved, a thoughtful gesture that warms a lonely heart.

A gift of time can be one of the most precious gifts anyone can share; time that can brighten up one's life even just for a brief moment. It leaves memories that will last until the next time.

Chapter 7
Comfort zone

The average person has dreams and aspirations for a better life, usually involving lifestyle and material objects. As we grow older and wiser, we may realise that there is more to life than material wealth. Finding purpose and meaning in life will eventually become the ultimate goal.

If you are 'normal', you have a comfort zone, generally considered a mental rather than a physical space. A reserved person will find it uncomfortable to start a conversation with a stranger, or someone afraid of snakes might not want to go on an Australian bush walk in summer. Countless behaviours thwart success in life by imprisoning you in your comfort zone.

As you move towards your goals, your comfort zone will challenge you every step of the way. It's just the Universe's way of PREPARING you to receive your desired outcome. Therefore, it's critical that you understand and master the concept of the comfort zone.

We are programmed to operate within our comfort zone. It acts as a protective barrier. It supposedly keeps us safe; it signals danger when we engage in strange behaviours like walking along the edge of a cliff with no safety barriers. While it serves a beneficial purpose, it also quickly outlives its usefulness by stifling growth and progress.

Humans are creatures of habit, but achieving your goals demands that you become more than you are now. It requires you to push and expand the boundary of your comfort zone thereby growing in 'consciousness'. It means doing things that you would not normally do, even taking risks or doing things that might make you look clumsy or foolish. It's precisely at these challenging moments where the real growth takes place.

Progress in life requires that you constantly confront and overcome challenging situations.

If you just wish and passively wait, your goals and dreams will fail to materialise. The key is to keep growing and expanding until you encompass your dreams, as depicted by the outermost circle in the diagram. You will then become in consciousness to a level that resonates and matches with your goals.

Goals push us towards new behaviours we'd rather avoid. Usually, it requires that we abandon old practices and adopt new ones. It can be quite a challenge for most people. It is one of the main reasons people don't achieve their goals.

Having a goal is a PLANNED CONFLICT with the comfort zone

It means leaving the familiar surroundings and exploring new territory. Sometimes exploring the new region can be exciting. Quite often it is daunting because you don't want to go the safety of your comfort zone.

To reach any significant goal, you must leave your comfort zone

Pushing through your comfort zone takes conscious effort and some risk. The inducement for staying in it is that you don't have to put in extra effort or take risks. However, the consequence of not pushing the boundary of your comfort zone is that you NEVER achieve your dreams. Understand that your dreams don't come to you; you must grow and expand until you encompass your ideas.

The comfort zone may be pushed gently or hard - you choose. However, the manner in which you push through will determine how quickly you grow and therefore how quickly you will achieve your desired outcome in life.

Realise that you are capable of MUCH more than you are demonstrating

It's true, not just positive thinking. But it takes an enormous amount of effort to push yourself to the limit... and merely reaching your ceiling is not good enough. You must dig deeper. If you want to get better, you must push past your limits, doing more than you THINK you can. It is where the real growth occurs. Don't only do your best; do what it TAKES.

There is a significant difference between doing your best and doing what it takes to reach your goal.

Our capacity to accomplish is only a state of mind. How much we can do depends on how much we THINK we can do. You have the ability within you to achieve just about any outcome you set for yourself, but you have to grow to manifest that outcome. Growing requires that you challenge yourself and endure prolonged periods of discomfort. However, the end will justify the means; the rewards will be worth it.

It is your choice as to which nature will dominate

Every person we know who can live life on their terms has consistently pushed the boundaries of their comfort zone, accepting full responsibility for their success.

Taking yourself out of your comfort zone is not a choice if you want to continue to grow, develop and be healthy as you age. "Use it or lose it" used to be enough, but now the research shows that we have to keep our brains and bodies active and learn new things continuously to combat the diseases of aging. Stepping out of your comfort zone enables you to live a longer, healthier and fuller life overall.

There are, however, many people who will do anything to stay within their comfort zones. In fact, it is estimated that many people never venture further than 50 miles from the place where they were born, and less than 25% of Americans own a US passport. Travelling is only one of many ways to expand your comfort zone. The important thing isn't what you do, but that you do something to develop yourself.

The reward of stepping out of your comfort zone is you feel alive and full of new energy. The more you step-out, the more comfortable and competent you become.

Your comfort zone is comprised of 4 distinct areas:

Place: If you are in a position or environment you have never been, you may be out of your comfort zone. Grow and learn through travelling, putting yourself in new situations, attending networking meetings, and enjoying different physical environments.

Proust said, "The real voyage of discovery consists not in seeking new landscapes but in having new eyes." Living in France and travelling made everything we saw new, different, and exhilarating. We felt like children in a candy store when we walked down a cobblestone street or stared up at an ancient church built in the 10th century. Travel and putting yourself in a new environment for a day, a week, a month, or for a year is a liberating and life-changing way to move out of your comfort zone.

People: Venture out to meet and interact with different people you don't know; go to a lecture, a networking meeting, travel, volunteer, attend a class or a party with the purpose of meeting new people.

Jean pushed himself out of his comfort zone while conducting his PhD research. He reached out to a professor at the Universite' Montpellier and asked for her assistance. As a result, he was able to involve her in the project and conduct the study with both US and French subjects.

Pursuits: If you continue to engage in activities you are familiar with and competent at, you are in your comfort zone. Once you start a new sport, skill, or event that you don't know, you move out of your comfort zone.

As a family, we would continuously venture out to new towns and villages and explore the countryside. These adventures pushed us out of the known and into areas that challenged us. Our senses were all on high alert from reading the roadmap to deciding the best place to eat lunch or go for a hike. Travelling afar is momentous, and yet we found driving 60 kilometres to a new village or region was equally as exhilarating.

Power of the brain: Completing tasks you are familiar with keeps you in your comfort zone and stretching yourself to try a new skill or work takes you outside of it.

Our brains are being stretched continually with learning the new social marketing tools. We have decided. However, we can't learn all of them at once, but one new one a month until we feel comfortable seems to be a good pace and keeps us growing.

Why don't we step outside our comfort zones more often?

We are still functioning on old innate primate instincts that tell us to play it safe, stay with the herd and protect ourselves from possible danger. It was important at one time, but no longer serves us today.

To grow and develop you have to step outside your comfort zone into the global world, we now live in. As children, we are programmed to grow and develop, but as adults, we have the choice to stagnate or continue to learn. If you desire to change anything in your life; to create more joy, better health, and pursue your dreams, you have to step outside your comfort zone and continuously challenge yourself to new adventures so that you can learn and grow.

A quick guide to stepping outside your comfort zone

1. Take small steps

Pick one or two domains in which you are willing to step outside your comfort zone.

Decide, for example, and you want to learn how to knit and to take a class with all strangers. What is the worse thing that would happen? You stab yourself with the knitting needle, and someone laughs at you. But wait, if it is a beginner's class, they won't know how to knit either, and the teacher is sure to show you how to handle the needles correctly.

2. Stick to it until it becomes comfortable

Keep going to the knitting class until it becomes so comfortable and you have learned everything you need to know to knit. Before you know it, you are signing up for the more advanced class, trying a more difficult pattern.

3. Repeat the process over and over and over again

As you practice stepping out of your comfort zone, you will find that you become bolder and courageous and want to try out new things. Try it in another domain; travel to an unfamiliar place, learn a new skill, develop a new relationship with someone who takes you out of your comfort zone.

4. Find the joy in stepping out of your comfort zone

Acting on your dreams, desires, goals, and wishes will all make you move out of your comfort zone. If you want to create the life you hope for, keep on practising moving out of your comfort zone. Before you know it, you will become captivated with the joy and feeling of accomplishment it brings to you.

Humility a true greatness

Humility starts from a position of dignity, strength and a healthy sense of your worth and abilities. A greatness that is rarely demonstrated, and a topic that can be redefined as a significant pursuit to improve your relationships, reduce stress & increase happiness both at home and in the workplace.

The Power of Humility takes you from being impoverished emotionally and spiritually to invisible wealth; serenity and peace. You must have the humility to grow, change, heal and help others.

Pride is concerned with who is right. Humility is concerned with what is right.

Pride is the opposite of humility and rages a battle deep within every heart. It is the engine of mediocrity because the proud think they have "arrived" and have nothing left to learn, probably not from you or me anyway.

When we bring up things in a conversation to make us look right in the eyes of others, it is a manifestation of pride. One recurring issue is talking too much, and name-dropping is a hidden form of pride being released.

To choose peace over conflict, a person has to be grounded in an accurate sense of self, with that comes to confidence and strong spiritual power, because you are not easily swayed by other's invitation to fight.

To get peace in your daily life, achieve levels of awareness, consciousness and relationship skills, which help you to get free of many of your conflicts. We must learn how to weaken the perils of pride and cultivate the promise of humility.

Why is humility better than tolerance?

Humility will CHANGE YOUR PERSPECTIVE AND ATTITUDE to help you come together with others in understanding. It reminds me of the power we attain when we let go and surrender. Humility doesn't seek to be known or celebrated. It aims to serve, make others better.

The ancient world admired honour, not humility, but what we need in the world now is Humility Revolution. We can learn many things from those living in extreme poverty, and it's simple. Humility inspires and lifts those around us, generating learning and growth, and provides a firm basis for self-esteem.

Humility isn't a position of weakness. Try making people feel important daily rather than yourself and see the strength it takes. Humility has nothing to do with the insecure & inadequate.

The root of everything good is patience, humility, honesty and respect, often translated into company core values through mission statements, business objectives and recruiting new employees. Money may make people rich, and knowledge could make people wise, but Humility makes excellent people, as well as excellent employees, great wives, husband, mothers, fathers, brothers, sisters and friends.

Human attributes are numerous. These attributes are positive as well as negative. A positive quality is reasonable and fruitful for humanity, while a negative characteristic is irrational and harmful to humanity. Attributes are required at all levels of human interactions, both individual as well as collective. The prominent positive human qualities that give a reasonable/beneficial shape to human personality or individuals are faith, knowledge, wisdom, good-manners, stability, justice, gratitude, courage, enthusiasm, and humility. These attributes are inter-linked with each other and mutually reinforcing. It is noteworthy, the absence of positive characteristics in human personality make room for negative characteristics such as doubt, ignorance, stupidity, bad-manners, volatility, injustice, jealousy, fear, grief, and pride. The negative traits are, too, interdependent and mutually reinforcing. The negative attributes give irrational/destructive shape to mindset/personality. The interconnected nature of characteristics and developmental approach of individuals regarding attributes' growth leads, ultimately, towards positive/negative mindset or wise/unwise personality profile. It is noteworthy that there is the innate tendency of extremism or perfectionism towards attribute development or continuation. A perfectionist or extremist tendency can pervert a positive attribute into a negative attribute; consequently, the approach brings failures/troubles in one's life. A pro-active and non-perfectionist approach is required to develop or to uphold multiple attributes at a reasonable level.

Humility divine perspective

Divine perspective is inevitably attached with personal humility. Man is weak by nature and unable to live or survive without some external support, both human as well as natural. The creator is neither humble nor liable to humility, but He likes humility of man and descends His Mercy due to the submissive posture of humanity, a vital cause of Divine Mercy. A person without humility behaves like the creator, especially at some critical moments of life struggle. Apparently, it is not a tenable situation, one has to face conseqences of pride, and humiliation is imposed on false god / proud man. It is noteworthy that humility is the vital cause of Divine Mercy, while satisfaction is a decisive factor for Divine Wrath.

Definition

Humility is hard and odious to define due to the presence of egoism/pride. Pride may distort the definitional effort, too. Our definitional attempt is based on Objective Analysis of human behaviour and Divine Guidance on the subject. Humility is state of mind that gives meekness to one's attitude.It reflects at the time of learning through hearty acceptance of some truth, manifests at the time of interaction through courtesy, reveals at the time of success through gratitude, and noticeable at the time of crises through patience. Pride is diagonally opposite to humility, and it is a negative trait of personality. Pride has two dimensions conceptual as well as practical. Conceptual ego has multiple aspects such as rejection of scientific truth, defiance of an intuitive truth, despising people, and superiority complex. These are prominent aspects of conceptual pride. The conceptual pride must activate practical pride. At practical level of pride, a person misbehaves or humiliates and speaks impolitely during interactions.

It is difficult, sometimes, to distinguish an intuitive or practical or conceptual truth from falsehood. The humble approach to unearth some absolute reality is to apply cause analysis on events/ideas/emotions. It is noteworthy, an intuitive truth is ultimately compatible with scientific facts, and practical truth is always beneficial for humanity. Moreover, an essential event creates inner satisfaction and makes someone altruistic. Humility creates, thus, appreciation for self and comforts for others.

Inner bases of humility

Man is, though, a complexly evolved phenomenon, however, nicely designed by nature. A man has two aspects, material as well as spiritual. It is the epitome of Divine creation. God created humanity with great mercy and affection. The very basis of human nature is, thus, the strong tendency of love and attraction towards Divine Attributes for self-perfection or purification. The natural trend towards Divine Attributes develops humility in one's personality.

Every individual is a unique combination of body, mind, and soul. Body, mind, and soul are best in stature & proportion and excellent in working & operation. At the physical level, the human body follows some environmental rules. These rules are countless. They are working patterns to maintain normal body functions. There is continuous improvement in physical sciences; consequently, new physical laws are unearthed, now and then. Every discovery in physical sciences makes humanity more commanding on natural forces and brings to light the significance of standard body functions. The human body is disturbed, generally, due to some physical lusts such as over-eating, lethargy, drinking, and smoking. At a psychological level, mind anatomy is at work for persistent peace of mind. Mind dispositions play an essential role in making, shaping, sustaining, and maintaining a mindset. An individual's perception is disturbed or behaves abnormally due to a negative mindset. At the spiritual level, soul phenomenon plays her role to shape a particular personality profile for eternal and everlasting growth and survival. The soul is conscious energy that has some definite directions; soul movement is perverted due to lusts/false beliefs. A structural and proportional profile of man set a normal/humble route for life activities; consequently, humility can be maintained, quickly, at all occasions by following the natural pattern of life activities.

Development of pride: A personality profile is the outcome of physical, psychological and spiritual leanings. At the physical level, instincts/needs are the basis for a personality profile. The prominent instincts/needs are food, clothing, shelter, sex, knowledge thrust, social interaction, and self-esteem. At a psychological level, mind powers/ bits of intelligence are the basis of personality profile. The mind has three essential bits of intelligence perceptual intelligence, emotional intelligence, and intentional intelligence. At the spiritual level, spiritual urges/senses are the basis of personality profile. The human soul has three significant senses religious reason, moral sense, and aesthetic sense. The divinely gifted bases of personality profile impose natural limits on human pride. However, proud creeps in and breeds healthy behaviour at the physical level, negative mindset at the psychological level, and isolation at a spiritual level. A healthy attitude at physical level creates multiple physical abnormalities such as fat, high cholesterol, blood pressure, diabetes, and fatigue. The cynical mindset at psychological level creates many psycho abnormalities such as tension, anxiety, depression, stress and strain. An isolated attitude at spiritual level develops dogmatic beliefs and behaviour pattern based on an unfounded system of rites and rituals. Life becomes irrational/immoral, consequently, many totems & taboos become part and parcel of daily life. Also, vulgarity and nudity rise due to the wrong elucidation of aesthetic sense. The outcome of pride is, thus, the presence of abnormal attitude at all levels of life physical, psychological, and spiritual.

External bases of humility

The external profile of a person is assessed during interaction with fellow human beings. Human interaction has three aspects - social, economic, and political. A proud person is discourteous during social interaction, exploitative during the economic interaction, and unjust during the political communication. On the other hand, a humble person is courteous during all types of social interactions, fair during multiple economic interactions, and moderate during numerous political interactions. A proud person is a narcissist or self-centred. The universal truth he follows is unfounded, the economic behaviour he manifests is irrational, the political attitude he depicts is dictatorial. The ultimate result of baseless/proud attitude at the corporate level of life creates turmoil at the social level, injustice at the economic level, chaos at the political level; the eventual outcome is the humiliation of proud person an arrogant nation. Hitler is a glaring example of proud attitude at the collective realm of life. His attitude and dictatorial decisions imposed countless humiliations on his nation. The humiliation mechanism works owing to interdependent nature of attribute phenomena and universality of the law of rewards & retribution. It is noteworthy that the law of reward & retribution works at all levels of life, individual as well as collective, and all types of human deeds, overt as well as covert. The only exception is non-infectious thoughts.

Individual life & humility

The ultimate aim of an individual is to live a contented and successful life. A happy life is free from conflicts, both internal as well as external. Life without internal conflicts provides inner satisfaction, and a life free from foreign disputes gives someone self-esteem at the collective level. The twin aims are easy to mention, however, difficult to achieve. There is the great and rampant presence of self-contradictory motives in inner self that makes someone muddled or depress. Similarly, self-esteem is a target hard to achieve. People, swollen with pride, are not ready to give someone self-esteem willingly instead confrontation is a frequent phenomenon of interactive life. People try to establish or demands self-confidence at the cost of the humiliation of others. Proud people get satisfaction from someone's embarrassment, they, ignore worth and value of others. However, humility helps the individuals to avoid negative infectious thoughts/tendencies of inner-self and makes room towards positive responses. Hearty gratitude for life achievements creates inner satisfaction, and enthusiastic acknowledgment of others' accomplishments builds self-esteem. It is noteworthy that appreciation and enthusiastic acceptance are acts of humility. The humble approach must create self-confidence a key to successful life.

Collective life & humility

Man is social entity. A man has a robust instinctual desire towards social interaction. Social interaction may take multiple shapes such as family interaction, tribe interaction, neighbourhood interaction, economic interaction (e.g., buying and selling interaction), and political interaction (e.g., vote casting and vote convincing communication). These interactions are incredibly complex and highly intricate. They are difficult to understand and ordeal to implement, properly. A mistake at a conceptual or practical level may lead towards some long-lasting or permanent miscommunications among individuals. Miscommunication at the corporate level is more horrible as compared to own misconceptions. A misconception at a state level is the worst form of collective miscommunication. It may lead towards some practical strife or war. A humble approach is a panacea to avoid any miscommunication at all levels, individual as well as collective. Real humility is shaped by humanistic tendencies towards others. Otherwise, hypocrisy is strengthened. Hypocrisy is courtesy without humble mindset. A little mentality with soft communication develops a charisma in a leader. A vast majority of people attract towards charismatic leadership for better and quick solutions to their problems.

Entrepreneurship & humility

Entrepreneurship is effective communication / negotiation. Communication is required at all levels of entrepreneurial struggle. It is required at the time of business initiation to attract lucrative investment opportunities, it is needed at the time of business development to hiring better (efficient & effective) staff, it is indispensable at the time of practical start for better initial image, it is inevitable on all occasions of business interaction for stable customers/stakeholders, it is unavoidable during multiple business operations in order to avoid mismanagement at all level of institutional struggle, and so on and so forth.

Effective communication/negotiation is directly and dynamically linked with politeness or courtesy, while courtesy is strongly linked with humility. A humble approach, thus, leads towards effective communication/negotiation inevitable pillars of entrepreneurial life.

A critical dimension of business decision-making process is projection / mirror-image of an entrepreneur. An entrepreneur's projection is the outcome of multiple personality traits such as confidence, enthusiasm, morale, and determination. Humility is the essence of these necessary traits of an entrepreneur. The absence of humility not only distorts the reflection of all positive traits but also indicates the presence of egoism, an extremely negative characteristic for entrepreneurs.

An entrepreneur trapped by egoism/narcissism reflects Managerial Ego. An egoist manager must fail in business life or entrepreneurial struggle. An egoist mindset is infectious and magnetises wise enemies and unwise friends, both are harmful to entrepreneurship, on the other hand, the humble mindset is charismatic and attracts wise friends.

Entrepreneurial struggle without humility creates some definite attitude at critical points of institutional conflict or interactions. For example, business courage without humility may convert into some brutality/exploitation of related economic agents, entrepreneurial confidence without humility can develop over-confidence, managerial morale without humility may lead towards careless/divergent decision-making process, executive determination without humility must establish inflexible attitude, administrative enthusiasm without humility can create humiliation for others during multiple institutional interactions, and so on and so forth. Consequently, it is impossible for related persons/stakeholders to take some encouraging decisions towards business interactions; as a result, failure is materialised due to Managerial Ego.

An entrepreneurial struggle is always succeeded due to teamwork. A successful team effort has two bases conceptual and practical. The theoretical basis is fortified due to some shared vision shared evenly among all members of a team, while the practical environ of unity is sustained due to discipline. A shared vision about institutional struggle is materialised by sacrificing a few individual beliefs, a conceptual submission/humility, and institutional control is actualised by sacrificing certain individualistic attitudes, a practical submission/humility.

5 keys to cultivate humility in life, love, and leadership

1. Each day end identify evidence of grace. The humble are frequently more persuasive and inspiring than the arrogant. We are more attracted to people who are modest than to those who are not. Keep a diary of grace to keep your ego in check.

2. Show respect to those you don't agree with. A humble person is marked by a willingness to hold power in service of others. Humility means treating those who hold contrary beliefs with respect and friendship.

3. Invite and pursue correction. Respond with ability doing this in humility. At times you will also be required to just forget about it, not responding at all. Leaving your ego aside useful if your journey is guiding you to harmony.

4. Act humbly, leave a legacy of greatness. Respond humbly to trials by encouraging others to be great. Give credit where it is due, openly or publicly where possible.

5. Lead by example. Provide those you influence with the tools of humility or show them the power of humility through your actions. Humility breeds inspiration and respect.

Chapter 8
The courage to live consciously

In our day-to-day lives, the virtue of courage doesn't receive much attention. Courage is a quality reserved for soldiers, firefighters, and activists. Security is what matters most today. Perhaps you were taught to avoid being too bold or too brave. It's also dangerous. Don't take unnecessary risks. Don't draw attention to yourself in public. Follow family traditions. Don't talk to strangers. Keep an eye out for suspicious people. Stay safe.

But a side effect of overemphasising the importance of personal security in your life is that it can cause you to live reactively. Instead of setting your own goals, making plans to achieve them, and going after them with enthusiasm, you play it safe. Keep working at the stable job, even though it doesn't fulfil you. Remain in the unsatisfying relationship, also though you feel dead inside compared to the passion you once had. Who are you to think that you can buck the system? Accept your lot in life, and make the best of it. Go with the flow, and don't rock the boat. Your only hope is that the currents of life will pull you in a favourable direction.

No doubt there exist real dangers in life you must avoid. But there's a massive gulf between recklessness and courage. I'm not referring to the heroic courage required to risk your life to save someone from a burning building. By courage, it means the ability to face down those imaginary fears and reclaim the far more powerful life that you've denied yourself. Fear of failure. Fear of rejection. Fear of going broke. Fear of being alone. Fear of humiliation. Fear of public speaking. Fear of being ostracised by family and friends. Fear of physical discomfort. Fear of regret. Fear of success.

Dimensions of courage

To recognise courage, it helps to distinguish the various facets of courage. Some of us manifest certain types of courage well but come up short in other areas. Try to detect which elements you exhibit and which need to be unleashed in your life.

- **Spiritual courage**. The spiritual journey requires being in the present. It is a trust in faith that propels you to continue growing. You become a "witness" to your attachments to results and learn to self-correct. You surrender your ego to a higher level of courage consciousness, and you begin to exist in a place "where courage meets grace." As all this happens, humility steps in to replace arrogance and righteousness. The sacred within awakens.

- **Emotional courage.** Similar to spiritual courage, this involves "knowing thyself." A path committed to contemplation is required to release your false identity. Thomas Keating in Open Mind, Open Heart defines it this way: "the self-image developed to cope with the emotional trauma of early childhood which seeks happiness in satisfying the instinctual needs of survival/security, affection/esteem, and power/control, and which bases its self-worth on cultural or group identification." In the Enneagram, it would relate to the instinctual fears around the three subtypes: social, one-on-one and self-preservation.

- **Leadership courage (individual and organisation).** The courageous culture of an organisation honours and uplifts the human spirit (the opposite of authoritarianism or coercion). The collective intent of a Braves organisation is to join hearts and minds to achieve inspired results. It means the organisation (and its people) will "fall on their swords" to honour their collective personal courage. Courage leadership knows the difference between pride and arrogance versus humility and grace.

- **Individual leadership courage.** Rooted in truth, you know your own heart, speak it appropriately and display dignity wedged with humility. People would label you courageous.

- **Ethical/moral courage.** This courage is activated by the attitude of willingness to choose differently in spite of personal hardship. The objective is a higher level of integrity than required for naturally alternative. Moral courage is like a compass. Ocean extended period, a one-degree navigational error will take you hundreds of miles off course.

- **Physical courage**. Facing a physical limitation that challenges the human body, utilising this to achieve athletic challenges, facing physical dangers or overcoming at serious health problems-these are the best-understood forms of courage today. Practising a contemplative life (stopping and "being") or being centred in mind, body and spirit are other less-known physical examples of courage.

- **Personal courage.** The way of your heart might be the easiest way to understand this form of courage. It is a blending of heart and mind combined with the commitment to hold yourself one hundred percent accountable for your actions. You must recognise that your spirit is the author of your fate such as feeling safe during times of uncertainty and feeling comfortable with the individuation of your mind it also contributes.

- **Political courage.** Unwillingness to sell your soul is the key feature, represented by whether you stand as a politician (self-serving) or political leaders (serving others). In other words, is your intention to do what is right for placing future needs ahead artisanal aspiration? Political courage is characterised by humility, not ego. It is being willed to go out on a limb to express an unpopular thought that reveals your authenticity.

- **Social courage.** Social courage exhibits congenial behaviour in public, regardless of the circumstance. With discipline and grace, you reveal a courage paradox: you do not insult others, nor do you suffer an offence in silence. Your image playa vital role, expressing the contradictory qualities of social grace with a rebellion against society's limitations.

By distinguishing and inserting these aspects of courage into your daily life, you increasingly manifest true courage, setting an example to which others can look for affirmation.

Tips to boost your courage

Seek courageous role models: Look around at the people in your life, in the media, in books, and in history. Who are your courageous role models? Learn about how they use their courage. Adopt strategies that appeal to you.

Collect courage quotes: Use the internet to find quotes about courage. Collect quotes that speak to you. Print some out, and post them where you'll see them.

Embrace your fear: Feel your fear. Practice sending compassion and understanding to yourself in your moments of fear. Sometimes just pausing with this intention is enough to release fear.

Admit to your fears with a friend: Sometimes it takes a lot of courage to admit we're afraid. Fear loves to hide in secrecy. Sharing your fears with an understanding friend or counsellor will usually help dispel some of the fear.

Don't engage the drama: By-pass worst-case scenarios. We never know what's going to happen, so why imagine the scariest possibilities? Fear feeds on drama and will multiply the more we engage. Practice stepping away from the scene, and imagining better-feeling scenarios.

Avoid unnecessary hesitation: The more you hesitate, the more your mind will interfere to tell you all the reasons why you should fret, worry, and not take that courageous action step you planned to take.

Commit yourself to advance: Schedule your courageous acts ahead of time. Then, show up.

Do it with a friend: Practice with a friend. Celebrate together as you take courageous action steps.

Start small: It can be hard to find the courage to do something that feels big and scary. Instead, take a good look at the big and frightening goal, and then break it down into smaller, friendlier steps.

Enter a state of non-resistance: Courage can be desperate to muster when we're dreading doing something. Practice letting goes of resistance and being present with whatever happens along your way.

Tap into your BIG WHY: Why do you want to use your courage? Get clear about your true, authentic intentions. When we feel inspired and motivated, sometimes we'll do just about anything to get what we want.

Visualize best outcomes: Visualization is a compelling technique to help us imagine our best outcomes. By visualising what you want, you will activate your reticular activator to help you begin to see evidence of what you're visualising. By allowing yourself to feel the energy of your imagined scene, you can boost both your enthusiasm and your courage.

Do things that others don't: Practice following the beat of your drum. The more comfortable you are doing your own thing, the more courage you will have to do anything.

Turn obstacles and failures into assets: It's easy to use obstacles and failures as excuses to forgo our courage. By turning obstacles and failures into opportunities to learn and grow, we can bypass fear and move forward with courage. It fortifies our courage to continue, despite obstacles or failures along our way.

Expand your knowledge: Many times we're scared of what we don't know or understand. By increasing your knowledge about a particular area, you will increase your confidence and courage to explore areas you might previously have avoided.

Incremental exposure: Little by little, expose yourself to the thing that you fear.

Imagine how you'll feel after you do it: Imagining how good you'll feel once you take action will boost your enthusiasm and your courage.

Exercise: Any form of exercise will help release pent-up stress and anxiety. Also, you will strengthen your sense of confidence as you follow through with regular use. Confidence nourishes courage.

Meditation: Meditation will help you feel centred, grounded, and relaxed. When you come from a place of centred calm, courage is much easier to access.

Affirmations: Affirmations, when frequently repeated, will assist your subconscious mind in helping you feel more courageous. Create a few short, easy-to-say, affirmations. For example: "I love feeling courageous." Or "My courage brings success." Repeat throughout your day, and for 2-5 minutes at a time. Remember -- repetition increases the power of an affirmation.

Heart breath: The heart breath will help you drop out of a worried, stressed mind, into the peace and wisdom of your heart. To do the heart breath, close your eyes and take a few long deep breaths. Next, continue to breathe deeply while imagining you are breathing in and out of your heart. Continue to breathe this way for 1-5 minutes.

EFT tapping: EFT Tapping, tapping on specific acupressure points on the face, torso, and hand, helps to reduce cortisol, the primary stress hormone. Calming your nervous system is an essential first step in cultivating courage.

Bad habits and self sabotage

It is no secret to the vast majority of us how we are to take care of ourselves. In fact when you think about it and get right to the meat of it is merely common sense. It orders to remain healthy in our bodies we should eat properly, get plenty of rest and exercise regularly. We know this. We also know that when we do this, we feel, or rather our bodies feel pretty fantastic. Why then is it that we will not gift ourselves with these things. You need no degree in advance education, no doctor, no one to tell you that every day you need to eat, to sleep, to move. The desire and need for these things come built into us from the moment of our conception, and it is our nature as a living organism. And so we do these things, but very often we do them in a way that is detrimental to ourselves. We take all of the fundamental needs that are built into us through our very nature as humans living in a body on a planet and corrupt them. We overfeed our bodies, overstimulate them and very often ignore them. Why do we do it? We do it because we have forgotten something else that is at the core of who we are, we are not just these bodies, we are so much higher than that. We are also part of what has created us, and we are part of divine creativity. We are connected to everything, and everything is connected to everything else. When we forget this, we feel as if we are empty, not whole but separate. We become so clogged up with all of the stuff that is external to us, which we sometimes think we are, that we can no longer feel any of the connection to our true selves.

Let us think about it like this, and everything is energy, everything. Your body, for instance, is made up of cells, which are made up of molecules, which are made up of atoms, which are made up of subatomic particles' and so it goes until you get to the smallest piece of what you and everything else in the universe is made of which is energy. Many of our planets great scientific minds have told us that energy cannot be created or destroyed. And so we are left with the understanding that it can only be transformed. Your body is made of energy that has been converted into you and when you die your cells will release that energy back into the energetic pool to be once again transformed into something else. It is a very 3-dimensional view of things but we are experiencing life in 3 dimensions aren't we?

Let's consider for a moment the types or forms of energy that we, in our disconnected bodies are being inundated by on a regular basis. We exist in information overload. We are bombarded daily by the news, the opinions of others, shoulds, musts and shoulds, email, texts, food choices, career choices, leisure choices, this list goes on and on. When we are in this state of feeling disconnected all of these forms of energy can become lodged in us. When we forget that we are directly connected to all that is we hold in us the thought that we are entirely responsible and for everything that is happening around us. We start to believe that we need to facilitate everyone else's happiness and that if we take the time and consideration to slow down and take a breath and take care of ourselves, we are doing something wrong, or not doing enough. And so the emptiness grows inside of us, because things out there in the world don't seem to get any better, in fact, they seem to get worse. We begin to try to fill that emptiness with food, with adoration, with television, with vacations and cars and clothes and with stuff. We start to feel defeated. The vacuum perpetuates the hole filling which makes us feel even more alone, shame-filled and separate. We pile stress on top of ourselves, more and more daily to try to ensure that we are working hard enough, that we are DOING enough. We don't want to get up off the couch and go for a walk out in nature; we forget to move our bodies because we learn from the world to live in our heads.

Remembering and feeling our connection to this divine creative source, remembering that we are part of what has created us is the door through which we can release the emptiness and disconnectedness that plague our species. Recognizing who we are, let me say that again, who we are is the pathway back to healthy bodies, minds and spirits. When this remembrance is sparked within us all of the common sense in a frame on planet things fall into alignment with it. Of course, we don't live on fast food and coffee, of course, we go out into the world and swim and dance and paint and build and create, of course, we nurture and accept one another, we don't know any other way to be. Once the trueness of who you are is remembered the energy that is you start to become unclogged, the experiences from the world around us that we held onto still occur but instead of being stuck inside our field they are allowed to pass through us and then out of us to be transformed once again into something else. We do not have to die to let this happen if we remember who we are we can remember that we, by our very nature are transformers of energy. Even at our most fundamental essential human functions, that is what we do. Once we knew this, children are born knowing this, and we educate it out of them. Ancient cultures knew this and still some cultures today do, and again we seem to want to teach it out of them. We have taken all of the great divine mystery of life and tried to strip it down into its parts. The universe is a perfect living organism, it is a whole, it is greater than the sum of its parts, and by looking at only pieces of it, we are missing the big picture as it were.

Regaining your remembrance of who you are is not an intellectual exercise. A hard pill to swallow given that fact that we place so much importance on intelligent things and processes. Our minds in their current stage of evolution will never be able to comprehend this connection. You will never understand it, and you will never be able to put it into words, you will only remember that you know it, that it feels like home. You no longer have a hole inside of you that needs to be stuffed full of things. You will see that you know that you know, that connection is part of who you are. That you are not just a separate body but you are the very source of creation experiencing itself. You will enjoy the energy of healthfully food and lifestyle because it matches your power, and you are drawn to each other in a way that your intellect will never be able to explain or comprehend. You won't even have to think about it at all it will just become a part of who you are.

As a society, we are continually baffled by why people perpetuate bad habits and self-sabotage, and we will continue to be confused by it. We are missing or ignoring the essential piece of life, and that is to live in the fullness of who we are and what we are here to do. Live. Experience. Transform energy. Add to the richness that is the divine creative force of the universe. We are not here to judge that experience. We are here to have it, and then let it be transformed. Let it come through us like water through a river system and then out into the ocean of creative force which cannot be created or destroyed. To begin to remember the fullness of our self we need to start to awaken and exercise it again. In the past, we had particular ideas on how to do this. Some of which included therapy, meditation, religion, lengthy, laborious processes and rituals, retreats, long periods of solitude, mental and physical suffering. In this new ear, we are being given many excellent teachers who remember how to awaken our remembrance of who we are without the old paradigms of the past. They can show us, using simple tools how to go directly to the source of that which we are a part of. Once we have known it, we cannot unknow it. The ability to go directly to our cause is still within us, and we just need a little help to flex our connectedness muscles as we have let them atrophy for generations. We no longer have to spend hours in meditation or years on a mountaintop to find ourselves and remember our divinity, that doorway has been reopened already funnily enough by the people who did those very things as our ancestors.

Many souls who have come forth today are holding that doorway open for the rest of us to step into the fullness of who we are. The hard work has already been done. We can remember how to reconnect in minutes, how to begin to awaken to the truth of who we are right now, this very second by merely acknowledging the fact that you are part of all that is and then feeling that in your body. Not thinking about it, because your mind can never understand, it's just too small. Just press it. By beginning to do this your energy will become less and less polluted, you will live much more healthfully and more abundantly.

No more excuses

Do you wish you could achieve your lifelong dreams by conquering no more excuses attitude and mindset? Are uncertain about the right technique that could ensure you with excellent results? Forget about your worries, and adopt a brilliant method that can help you towards personal development. With an efficient technique, eliminating excuses comes rather quickly, so you can tread the path towards success.

Get in touch with your deepest desires

Initially, you need to understand your primary goals and priorities in life. Upon realising what your purpose is, as well as your reason for establishing your goals, you can start creating a plan that will lead you towards your purpose in life. The more you understand your deepest desires and wishes, the more you can go onwards to achieving every item in your list. Hence, it takes complete awareness and understanding of your goals before you can begin creating a game plan for success.

Eliminate if's and but's

As soon as you start worrying and making excuses to fulfil your dreams, you will find yourself moving farther from the path of success. Hence, you may only see yourself caught up in a cycle of losing your purpose and conviction to achieving your intentions in life.

With this in mind, it makes sense to maintain a sense of determination and focus as you take each step towards your progress. Do your best to empower yourself, no more excuses and never compromise your beliefs just for the hopes of pleasing others. It may require considerable discipline and courage, yet the rewards of standing firm to what you believe in can yield excellent rewards.

The time is now

The fact is everyone can be a victim of lack of focus, and many people tend to put off a significant decision that can lead to life-changing effects. Unfortunately, high opportunities do not come by every day, so you should start chasing your success instead of sleeping on it and going against the inner voice that tells you to start moving now. As soon as you have a clear purpose and goal in life, you better act swiftly and take the right move towards it.

What it takes to win

Keep in mind that no one is born a winner, and it takes the right mindset, strong character and determination to find yourself in the midst of success. What you need to know is that every second, every minute, and every single day counts. You can make things happen as soon as you admit to yourself that you are capable of succeeding and start taking the right action that ensures your success. Thus, build your dreams, cut out the excuses, and make the right move now.

Setting a standard

In this world of establishing a life standard, it is hard to live without clearly defined boundaries and limits. Many times your integrity is tested, and to survive you need to set high standards. The price of living without measures is very dear, and therefore one cannot afford to lead an ignorant life especially in the current times.

Your character and values will be tested whenever you are facing a challenge. You need to be strong enough during trying times so that you do not compromise your principles and life standard. Temptations usually are very inviting, and you may tend to downplay their effects if your thinking is blurred by desire in the heat of the moment. But once you bend to the invitation, you will pay for regret so later.

The consequence of ignoring your life standard is usually very severe and can be detrimental to your self-esteem. Needless to say, on the other hand, if you resist temptation you will afterwards feel much stronger and confident. The best way of beating attractions is to make a point of always thinking more than once and making conscious, rational and responsible decisions.

You cannot, therefore, live without stated boundaries and limits as you will be shaped by the life standard you have set for yourself. Failure to establish boundaries and rules you will have low self-will and control. You will lose ambition and thus lack motivation leading to a gross letdown.

Success is a long-term outcome of individual discipline and commitment to your cause. A breach of your principles will cost you a lot.Nevertheless; it will be a double mistake if you fail to rise soon enough, after falling.

Wake up

Wake up with determination. Such a natural principle to live by and yet today, at this very moment, the matrix that is your mindset traps you. In truth, it is your belief system which is so ever-present. It keeps you from taking action and becoming who you want to become.

So, how can you have the correct mindset right from the start go? What are you going to accomplish today? How can you make progress? What can you do to achieve your goals? How can you help?

You must understand that your mindset is so ingrained into the fabric of who you are and the way you process data that you do not even notice it. You do not even know it is real. And that is a fact that impacts your life; it is your inability to see that your mindset controls everything you think, believe or do.

Therefore, if you want to wake up with determination, you can reconstruct your belief system. If you can choose at any moment to believe in something that is more empowering than what you thought the moment before, it finds its way into your actions. It allows you to do things you could not do previously knowing that opportunity is right now.

And to wake up with determination in the morning, you must take a few minutes to look or think about your goals. Then motivate yourself and think positive thoughts. The reason I am saying this is because as you awaken, your subconscious mind still accessible for the next twenty minutes which set the rhythm of your day. So, you have to choose what you think or say wisely.

Waking up with determination sets the pace

When you wake up with determination, no matter how much you appreciate life, or how much you are grateful for, you always make it better. It does not matter who you are, or what your goals are for the day. So do something that will help set you up for success that day.

Then the time comes to hustle! So, you will be happy you did, and you will be one step closer to your goal! If you do that, you will then go to bed with satisfaction! And if you live each day by waking up with determination, you will achieve your goals.

Now, while you strive for greatness or to accomplish desires, it also makes life a little more complicated. You have to realise that you are trying to make changes while you are living life. Thus, you seek to modify the course of energy which is already propelling you on a particular path.

Being determined by small changes

There are also people who decide to cut most or all ties with their past lives, jobs, habits, friends, and even countries. The majority, however, cannot risk losing everything to create the life of their dreams. Therefore, you perhaps have no choice than to live the life you are now living.

Waking up with determination is a choice

When you do not wake up with determination, you are dividing your beliefs, thoughts, and focus on the life you are trying to change and the one you are attempting to build for yourself. Some people do jump ship and start from scratch, but it is a choice.

Either way, you have to wake up with determination and do all that you can to go to bed with satisfaction. There is no other way to stay in the right frame of mind. And if you are not determined, you will inevitably fail.

The key to wake up with determination

So, the critical element is to end the day strong, and the only way is by starting it off with the right mindset. Rather than hitting your phone alarm or clock, you should take a minute or two to focus on your goal when you want to wake up with determination.

You have to focus, not dwell, on the goal that matters most to you, and this, first thing each morning and evening. Visualize you achieved your primary goal, and use that vision to fuel your day.

Determination is also taking risks

How many seconds and minutes do you waste every day doing things that do not even bring you near your goals, aspirations, and dreams? A determination is also taking risks which are at the core of your journey to success. You have no other choice than to jump into the unknown and see what happens.

Yes, of course, the risk is, somewhat, terrifying. You can lose everything you have in the process. Criticism and humiliation may also be a part of the encounter. All you have left after is to pick up the pieces and begin all over again, and often, more than once. The rewards can be prodigious, but so can the cost. You will fail, but you will have to rise. So, in all cases, your asset is to wake up with determination.

Risk and the will to win

When you wake up with determination, all will chip away at your will to win. So, ignore that weak voice inside of your mind which is telling you that you won't be able to make it. It will beg you to stop and promise safety and security if you would just quit. And yes, if you leave, you are not at risks anymore, but you are also not at possibilities for greatness.

If you want to achieve something, you have got to find ways to put yourself at risk for something significant to happen. You have to put yourself in the situation where you may fail. People will have doubts and say that you have limits, but those boundaries are self-placed by the same individuals. The reason is that they were not willing to take a risk or they failed. But you can go beyond that.

As a result, if you are not waking up with determination, courage, taking risks and going to bed with satisfaction, you are missing out on a better, more pleasant reality for yourself.

Determination is essential

The key is that, if you want to make an extraordinary performance, or if you're going to dazzle people absolutely, then you have to do something unusual. You have to be willing to put yourself out there. And you need to do things that other people think are going to break you, or that others just believe there is no way that you could be able to pull that off.

You have to show that an ordinary human animal is incapable of going to the lengths which you are professing to go. And when you declare it, you have to be ready to back it up. You have to put yourself on that march knowing that under no circumstances or reason whatsoever, you'll ever be willing to back down.

When you wake up with determination and go in with that level of certainty, then and only then, you are going actually to pull it off.

Being determined builds momentum

So, you have to wake up each day with determination. In this way, you can build momentum, because without it you will never realise your goals. A lot of people underestimate the importance of momentum. You need it to produce the well-needed power and energy to break through whatever walls and obstacles life has placed in your way.

No matter how small, rejoice in every success you get along the way. Use it to fuel your drive and desire to succeed. Exploit it to push yourself onward with even more resilience. You might fail at times, but use your failures to give you more determination to reach even greater success.

If you wake up with determination and go to bed with satisfaction, you will always feel proud to live the existence you currently live. I do not fear many things in life, but regrets, they stick with you. It only hurts you and drags you down.

4 steps to wake up with determination

To wake up with determination, take an hour or two, and go in nature. Sit there and write down your five top goals and dreams. However crazy your goals are, just write them down. Think of what you want to be written on your tombstone and what you would like to be remembered for?

Then put a dash that says 'next step,' because the most significant problem people have is that next step. We can all write down our passion, but we always struggle with the next step. And right down next to your goals, put the resources you already have that you can use.

Next thing to do is to print what you have written and posted it. Post it in three places, where you go to bed, where you brush your teeth, and on the door, you go in and out the most in your house. And the reason why is that, your home is your sanctuary, it is the place you trust.

Keep looking at those posts for as many days and months as you possibly can. And you will start to believe and wake up with determination. What you think becomes your reality. But how can that be? Belief itself is a construct, and if a conviction is such, then it can be manipulated and changed.

A final word

At any moment, and this is important to understand, you can choose to believe something new about yourself. The soon as you change a belief, it becomes real. I do not know why or how that is, and I may never understand it but after some time, just believing something makes it right.

You have to live the life you were born for because if you do not, you will regret it. If you learn something or if you take away one thing from this book, it should be: create your reality and always remember that luck is an accumulation of superior efforts and focused execution. Therefore, you should ever wake up with determination and go to bed with satisfaction.

www.ingramcontent.com/pod-product-compliance
Lightning Source LLC
Chambersburg PA
CBHW070201230526
45471CB00002B/772